The First War of the United States:

The Quasi War with France

1798-1801

The First War of the United States:

The Quasi War with France

1798-1801

by

William J. Phalen

Vij Books India Pvt Ltd
New Delhi (India)

Published by

Vij Books India Pvt Ltd
(Publishers, Distributors & Importers)
2/19, Ansari Road
Delhi – 110 002
Phones: 91-11-43596460, 91-11-47340674
e-mail: vijbooks@rediffmail.com
web : www.vijbooks.com

To one and all, Maureen, Hilary, John, Cassia, Callan, Jane, Brendan, Megan, Gia, Maggie, and the other creatures that have fur and fins.

Contents

Preface

As the title indicates, this book is the story of a little known conflict between the United States and France soon after the founding of the American nation. The conflict is important because of the involvement of the United States not only in another war almost immediately after its revolution, but also the new nation's attempt to find its way in dealing with international situations.

During the period of the French Revolution and the European wars, neutral nations, especially the United States, because they had the largest share of the Atlantic carrying trade, should have gained enormous profits. Unfortunately, this was not the case, in fact the reverse was true, neutral commerce suffered severely at the hands of the different belligerents.

In a message to Congress on December 6, 1793, President Washington called attention to these facts, asking those who had suffered losses to furnish proof that measures might be taken to redress their grievances. Early in 1894, a group of Philadelphia merchants submitted a list of their losses with proof adding, "It has become a practice for many of the privateers of the belligerent powers to send into port all American vessels they meet with, bound from any of the French ports in the West Indies to the United States; . . . and though many of these vessels have been afterwards liberated, yet the loss by plunder, detention, and expense is so great as to render it ruinous to the American owner."[1]

---

1   Gardner W. Allen, *Our Naval War with France* (Boston, Houghton Mifflin, 1909), p. 28-29

The Quasi War was a direct outgrowth of the French Revolutionary Wars. In 1778, during the American Revolution, the United States and France signed treaties of alliance and commerce. In 1792, the French Revolution precipitated a general European war, and the following year Great Britain joined France's continental enemies. Although still allied to France, was determined to avoid being drawn into this conflict.

The French had no objection to American non-intervention as long as the young republic clearly tilted its foreign policy towards France. Instead President George Washington in 1793 issued the Neutrality Proclamation, which warned Americans "to adopt and pursue a conduct friendly and impartial toward belligerent Powers."[2]

In 1794, the United States went further by signing the Jay treaty with Great Britain which, while not the American intention, caused two problems for the French. First, the they were convinced that the treaty was a betrayal of the Franco-American alliance and secondly, the trade that the American nation had with France, now basically went to England, tripling American exports to that country by 1801.

Because of these developments, In 1796, France attacked American commerce, attempting to force the United States to repudiate the Jay treaty. The United States, protected by the Atlantic Ocean and the British navy, rebuilt its own navy, and defended it self, leading to what became known as the Quasi War, an undeclared conflict fought entirely at sea, that neither nation wanted.

2   Proclamation of George Washington, April 22, 1793

Introduction

With the end of the American Revolution, the United States began to profit from its trade with European nations, begun when it was a colony of Great Britain. By 1893 however this trade was interrupted by a continuation of the long standing enmity between England and France.

In 1778, the Treaty that the United States signed with France obligated each of the two nations to support one another if either went to war with England. When war came however, the United States fearing that it was too weak to wage war against England did not support the French. President Washington issued a proclamation in 1793 which spelled out the attitude of the United States towards the warring countries declaring that the United States will "pursue a conduct friendly and impartial toward the belligerent powers." Further, to the dismay of the French in 1795, the United States and Great Britain signed what became known as Jay's Treaty. Many of the terms of the treaty had to do with finally settling issues remaining since the Treaty of Paris which ended the American Revolutionary War, however the French believed that this agreement joined the United States to Great Britain, an agreement that would be against French interests. "In vain we have hoped for some time that gratitude, or at least self-interest, would make of that federal republic a loyal ally of France. Now Washington [President] has concluded with our most implacable enemies a treaty wholly inimical to our interests."[1]

Given this situation, the French began looking upon the United States as, if not an enemy, then as an offending neutral, which

---

1   Durand Echeverria, *Mirage in the West: A History of the French Image of American Society to 1815* (Princeton: Octagon Books, 1957), p. 218

allowed commanders of French war vessels power to take cargoes on American ships, impress American seamen, and seize American ships as prizes.

How had this situation come about? When the first news of an armed revolt of the British colonies in America reached France, its potential impact was immediately assessed by the French government. At this time, England was not only a traditional opponent of France, but also, a growing economic competitor. Against France, the British were able to make up for her smaller population by almost permanent coalitions with other European powers and through an aggressive colonial expansion resting on a strong navy. The French King, Louis XVI and his secretary for Foreign Affairs, Comte de Vegennes made the decision to intervene in America when they received a report from their secret envoy, chevalier de Beaumarchais, who had been dispatched to Philadelphia in the fall of 1775. This report stating that "The patriots have decided to proclaim their independence and fight fiercely for it," was received in Paris the following February.[2]

On May 2, 1776, Louis XVI and Vergennes ordered Beaumarchais to create a company known as RoderiqueHortalez to which Vergennes wrote:

> "....We will give you a secret one million [Livres]. We will endeavor to persuade the court of Spain to give you another. With these two millions you shall find a great commercial establishment, and, at your own risk and peril, you shall furnish to American arms and everything else necessary to sustain war. Our arsenals will deliver to you arms and munitions, but you will pay for it...."[3]

In July 1776, Congresses envoy, Silas Deane is introduced to Beaumarchais and requests arms and clothing for 30,000 men, by

2 *France's Contribution to American Independence*, prepared by M. Jacques de Trentinian, for a filmed DVD educational program for the Sons of the American Revolution. August 2, 2013

3 Ibid.

September the following arms and equipment are assembled for shipment to America:

- 300,000 pounds of powder

- 30,000 rifles

- 3,000 tents

- 200 cannon + carriages + limbers

- 27 mortars

- 100,000 cannon balls

- 13,000 bombs

- 40,000 yards of lining for pants and pockets

- 30,000 blankets

- 180,000 aunes (1.2 yards) of cloth for soldier's shirts

- 18,000 aunes of cloth for officers' shirts

- 120,000 dozens of buttons for soldiers

- 18,000 dozens of buttons for officers

- 30,000 woolen caps

- Knives, handkerchiefs, shoes, garter claps

- 95,000 aunes of fabric for the soldier's uniforms

- Plus 12,000 cubic feet of wood for ship building

The French also send a little over one hundred officers, among them are: Louis Lebeque Du Portail who will become the chief military engineer of the Continental forces throughout the war; Baron VonSteuban the drill master of the American army; the former head of Louis XVI's secret diplomacy; Baron de Kalbwho would command troops during the fighting in the South; and most famously, Marquis de La Fayette, a favorite of George Washington.

The French influence on the outcome of the American Revolution continued into the war's final battle at Yorktown, Virginia in October 1881, where the French fleet under Comte de Grasse trapped the British army between his fleet and the American army comprised of 8,800 American and 7,800 French troops and forcing them to surrender to George Washington. Most historians would agree that without the French assistance to the American cause would have been lost.

A study of the Quasi War, could be looked upon from several viewpoints. As a war, as a study of war and peace, or as a look at the effect of this conflict upon the new American nation and the actions it took to deal with it. I have chosen the latter because of the events that happened in the short space of time that the war lasted, both militarily and diplomatically.

Chapter 1

The United States and France After the American Revolution

On October 6, 1777, the American military forces defeated a British army at Saratoga, New York. While this was a major military victory for Britain's former American colonies, its importance was amplified because soon after on February 6, 1778 a defensive treaty was signed between the United States and France. The French supported the new nation mainly because with this victory at Saratoga, the Americans could possibly defeat the British and France's influence would weaken the British and gain a measure of revenge for its defeat in the French and Indian War.

Between 1778 and 1782, the French provided supplies, loans, arms, and ammunition and at the war's final battle at Yorktown, Virginia, troops and naval support allowed the colonials to defeat the British. With this victory, the Americans entered into peace negotiations with the British, presenting a united front with the French in spite of British attempts to drive a wedge between the allies. The negotiations ended with the Treaty of Paris signed on September 3, 1783.

The aid that France gave to the United States was given openly under the terms of the Treaty of Alliance, which also recognized the United States of America. Beginning in the spring of 1776 however the French began to support the Americans covertly. Most of this aid was in the form of gunpowder. In addition, French ports accommodated American ships including privateers and Continental Navy warships that attacked British merchant ships. France also provided significant economic aid, either as donations or loans, and in addition offered technical assistance, granting some of its military strategists "vacations," so they could assist American troops.

Among them was Pierre Charles L'Enfant and most notably, Lafayette who became an aide to Washington and a combat general who also provided a legitimacy for the war giving confidence that that there was serious European support for American independence.

Equal to any other reason for the French to back the American cause was the presence of Benjamin Franklin in Paris. Franklin arrived in 1776 as Ambassador, a post he would hold until 1785. He conducted the affairs of his country with great success, which included securing the critical military alliance in 1778. Much of this he accomplished by developing and befriending a network of important French scientists, even having them elected to the American Philosophical Society of Philadelphia.

Additionally, he continued to develop his network of influential friends in France through the French Masonic network, and the aristocratic salons where he became extremely popular. To understand Franklin's popularity among scientists and non-scientists alike, one must remember that, although France was still an absolute monarchy, many liberal thinkers, even in the aristocracy, considered that the fight of the colonists was worthwhile and echoed their own questioning of France's political and social system. They were interested in the American struggle as it was framed in the universal values of the Enlightenment which they shared, such as equality and liberty. As a result, volunteers flocked to Washington's army: at first the American population was not very cordial towards these papist soldiers, but soon warmed to them. American liking for the French thus started to develop and was fueled by the intense Anglophobia that the war was bound to elicit through the depredations of British troops such as the destruction of plantations in the South. By 1783 French-American friendship could be considered as a genuine mutual fascination, affecting citizens and subjects in all walks of life and boding well for the future.[1]

However, there was debate in the American Congress as to why the French would stand with them against the British. First, it would be a mistake to attribute the French support of America exclusively to a feeling of revenge for the humiliations of the prior war against England.[2] Other motives came in and exercised a decisive influence. There was a conviction, and a right one, in France and the United States that for Britain to hold under control the whole of North America as well as India would give her a maritime supremacy, as well as a superiority in wealth, which would constitute a standing menace to the rest of the civilized world. There was also an enthusiasm among the young nobility in France and among officers in the American army, which, even aside from the bitterness towards Britain with which it was mingled, had great effect, and to this was added the sympathy of doctrinaire political philosophers who then and for some time afterwards had great power in forming French public opinion. . . But above this, was the sense of right which was uppermost in the breast of the unfortunate sovereign[3] who then, with little political experience but high notions of duty as well as of prerogative, occupied the throne. "The king," said Franklin, when writing to Congress on August 9, 1780, "a young and virtuous prince, has I am persuaded, a pleasure in reflecting on the generous benevolence of the action in assisting an oppressed people, and proposes it as a part of the glory of his reign."[4]

The three representatives who signed the Treaty of 1778 on behalf of the United States; Benjamin Franklin, Silas Deane, and

---

1   *French-American Relations in the Age of Revolutions: From Hope to Disappointment (1776-1800)*, Speech given on February 6, 2003 by Marie-Jeanne Rossignol, Professor of American Civilization, University Paris 7

2   The French and Indian War

3   Louis XVI

4   A Century of Lawmaking for a New Nation: U.S. Congressional Documents and Debates, 1774-1875, The Revolutionary Diplomatic Correspondence, Volume 1, Introduction, Chap. 4, p. 43

Arthur Lee reported afterwards that in the negotiations, the French made no effort to take advantage of the American situation versus Great Britain. Even though the United States was in great need, the French did not drive a hard bargain. The treaty was in fact drawn up as if the two powers had been of equal strength and equally in need of the alliance. The representatives also reported to Congress that they had every reason to be satisfied with the good will of the French court and of the French nation and hoped that Congress would accept the treaty.[5]

In their desperate straits, the Americans gladly signed the treaties[6] and assumed the obligations imposed upon them which in later years would prove embarrassing, but no serious trouble arose between the two nations until after the breaking out of the general European war brought on by the French Revolution in July of 1789.

One final reason for the French to initiate such a treaty with the United States was their certain realization that they would be going to war with Great Britain and whether it was better to meet it with America as a friend or with America united with England. "Shall we sleep in false security, and lose the one chance which may offer itself for centuries to reduce England to her true position? . . . Never was such an opportunity furnished to the House of Bourbon to lower the pride of her enemy, and to form with the United States an alliance of which the benefits should be incalculable."[7]

In supporting the American cause the French spent about 1.3 billion livres (approximately thirteen billion U.S. dollars) in direct support to America, not counting the money that it spent fighting Britain on land and sea outside the United States. Comparing the amount of money that France spent supporting the United States

---

5   Francis Wharton, *The Revolutionary Diplomatic Correspondence of the United States*, Government Printing Office, 1889, Volume ii, p.490

6   There were actually two treaties, one a treaty of amity and commerce, the other a treaty of alliance.

7   James Perkins, *France in the American Revolution* (Williamstown, Mass.: Corner House Publications, 2014), p. 241-242

against the benefits that it derived, this action was a pyrrhic victory. On the plus side, France gained some additional territory in North America and weakened its major enemy, Great Britain, but it gained no new European territory and the huge financial outlay severely degraded its' fragile finances and increased its' national debt. Perhaps another benefit would have been a fast growing trading partner in the United States, but this was not to be.

France paid a steep social as well as economic price for her participation in the American Revolution, according to Edmund Burke. Tens of thousands of French soldiers, sailors, and officers returned to France having witnessed individual liberties for the first time and bearing testimony to their benefits. As Burke put it:

They imbibed a love of freedom nearly incompatible with royalty. It seemed a grand stroke of policy to reduce the power and humble the pride of a great and haughty rival . . . for as it was universally supposed that the loss of America would prove an uncurable, if not a mortal wound to England, so it was equally expected that the power of the Gallic throne would thereby be fixed on such a permanent foundation as never again to be shaken by any stroke of fortune.[8]

In 1789, George Washington accepted the presidency, and after Washington himself, the leading spirit of his administration was Alexander Hamilton who he appointed secretary of the treasury. By the late 1780's the yearly interest payments on the national debt had reached $4.5 million. To deal with the debt, Hamilton's plan was to assume the debts of the states incurred during the war, refinance the nation's foreign debt, and to establish a sinking fund to buy securities selling below par value. The key to success however was commercial growth which in America was based on international trade and shipping. The Federalist Party became synonymous with the commercial trading economy. As a result the "merchant" became the central figure in this world. This was a person who at this time

---

8   Edward S. Corwin, *French Policy and the American Alliance of 1778* (Princeton: Princeton University Press, 1916), p. 375-376

owned very little on land, perhaps a retail store or a wharf, but always an ocean based entity – a ship, a share in a ship, and shares in the ship's cargo. Either an export or an import, manufactured products from Britain; sugar, coffee, and rum from the West Indies; and pepper, tea and spices from the Orient and East Indies. This trade led to more than trading. Because of the vagaries of the shipping business, losses due to the risks of weather, waves, pirates, and politics, the merchants became sophisticated financiers, moving from shipping into merchant banks and marine insurance. All of these entrepreneurs took advantage of the sea to amass wealth and respect.[9]

America's international presence was only through its merchant ships flying the stars and stripes. Because the United States had no navy. The last ship of the Continental navy was the frigate *Alliance* which had been sold in 1785 because Congress did not have the resources to maintain it, or to add to the fleet to create an effective navy.

Alexander Hamilton in Federalist Paper No. 11 recognized both the strategic necessity of a navy and what the Federalists regarded as the wholesome symbiotic relationship between maritime commerce and the navy. "[F] or influencing the conduct of European nations towards us," Hamilton wrote, "the establishment of a federal navy would be a central concern of government under the new Constitution. While a navy need "not vie with those of the great maritime powers," it should be of "respectable weight if thrown upon a scale" of the warring European nations, particularly for operations in the West Indies. Hamilton warned that without the Union, there would be no navy, and without a navy "our commerce would be a prey to the wanton intermeddlings of all nations at war with each other, who having nothing to fear from us, would with little scruple or remorse supply their wants by depredations on our property as often as it fell in their way. The rights of neutrality will only be respected when they are defended by and adequate power.

---

9   Douglas C. North, *The Economic Growth of the United States* (New York: W.W. Norton& Co., 1966), 46-53

A nation, despicable by its weakness, forfeits even the privilege of be neutral." The federal union could produce a navy and Hamilton predicted that each institution of the country would flourish in direct proportion to its support of naval force. "To this great national object, a navy," the Southern states would furnish durable timber and naval stores, the Mid-Atlantic States would supply the ironwork, and the New England states would produce the seamen. Simply put, maritime trade needed a navy, and the nation could build one.[10] Yet when the new government was established in 1789, it had no money for a navy and more pressing tasks at hand to even consider starting to construct ships.[11]

With the war for its independence over, the United States was faced with the prospect of dealing with two important foreign powers, the British with whom they had just waged war to gain that independence, and the French who made that independence possible with its loan and supplies of military products.

Earlier, colonial Americans had had a negative image of France. Americans shared the bias and prejudice of their English Anglican cousins against their frequent continental Catholic antagonists. A "remarkable detestation of the French . . . prevailed in America," one historian has written.[12] Another argued that prior to 1775, the stereotypical image of the French "suggested an incarnation of the Devil."[13] There is also the fact that the English settlers in the new world came basically in family units with the intention of becoming permanent residents of America. The French, for the most part, came as individuals, to hunt and trap, and then return to France. And finally that there was little interaction between the two groups,

---

10 Federalist 11, November 23, 1787

11 Frederick C. Leiner, *Millions for Defense, The Subscription Warships of 1798* *(Annapolis:* Naval Institute Press, 2000), p.10

12 Howard Mumford Jones, *American and French Culture*, 1750-1848 (Chapel Hill: University of North Carolina Press), 1927), p. 501

13 William C. Stinchcombe, *The American Revolution and the French Alliance* (Syracuse: Syracuse University Press, 1969), p. 2

the French settling inland in the wilderness areas and the English colonists residing along the East coast of America.

The French-American alliance against England in 1778, therefore, had marked a critical milestone in the relationship between France and the new American nation. "The initial reaction to the Alliance," represented "almost a complete reversal of previous America stereotypes.[14] Additionally, news of the French Revolution created a sympathetic bond on the part of the Americans to the country that had come to their aid in 1778. Americans looked upon the events in France as confirming and validating their own revolution.

In analyzing the French image of American society, there existed two levels of opinion. One was the body of popular or public opinion, the other the individual opinions of the French intellectuals. During the American Revolution, these two levels joined under the dominant ideas of Liberty, Virtue, Prosperity, and Enlightenment. The idea of progress made the basic assumption that man advanced toward intellectual, moral, economic, and political perfection in simultaneous and interdependent processes. Therefore American political achievements necessarily implied parallel moral, economic, and intellectual progression. No one could have better substantiated such an assumption than did Benjamin Franklin, who was at once a scientist, a moralist, and a politician, and who constantly preached the gospel of American prosperity and progress.

The idea of American liberty at first meant to the French merely the political independence of the colonies from England, and their support was at once an expression of Anglophobia and an admiration for a small nation asserting its national integrity. This was the kind of admiration which, in part at least inspired the French volunteers of 1776 and 1777.

But this championship of American liberty soon broadened into a championship of the rights and liberties of man, into the

14 *Ibid.* p.15

philosophic idealization of America as a land of freedom, equality, and toleration. Anne Robert Jacques Turgot, the French economist and statesman said in his praise of American liberty, "It is impossible not to hope that this people may attain the prosperity of which they are susceptible. They are the hope of the human race: they may well become its model."[15]

Early in its' revolution, American liberty came to signify to most Frenchmen not merely an overthrow of British political and economic control, but the revolt of an entire people against the tyranny of absolute power, a mass assertion of the inalienable rights of man. This idea was produced mainly by American political documents. The many pamphlets, constitutions, and bills of rights protesting against English interference and reaffirming already established and familiar rights and privileges sounded in French ears like the most radical and reactionary utterances.

Consequently, the extensive publication in France of translations of American political literature constituted a historical event of considerable importance. These works included the writings of Dickerson, Paine, Franklin and other American leaders along with reprints from American newspapers. The key documents were the various state constitutions, the Articles of Confederation, and the Declaration of Independence. The magazine Recueil des lois constitutives stated editorially, "These laws seem to me the finest monuments of human wisdom. They constitute the purest democracy which has ever existed: they already appear to be achieving the happiness of the people who have adopted them, and they will forever constitute the glory of the virtuous men who conceived them."[16]

The period between the Treaty of Paris in 1783 ending the American Revolution and the French Revolution in 1789 was one in which French good will towards America reached its fullest

15 "Lettre a Price," in Honore Gaberiel Riquetti, Comtede Mirabeau, *Considerations sur L'Ordre de Cincinnatus* (London, 1784) p. 199-200

16 Recueil des loisconstitutives, (Paris, 1778)

expression. This good will was engendered by popular enthusiasm and the strength of fraternal cooperation.

One of the most important results of the Treaty of Paris was that for the first time there was unrestricted communication between the United States and the non-British world. The flow of information from America to France, which had been a trickle, mainly coming indirectly through London, now became a comparative flood pouring directly across the Atlantic. English books and especially English newspapers were still important sources, but they were now secondary to the direct channels – the packet boat service to American ports started in 1793, the unrestricted movement of merchant ships and the development of French American trade, the establishment of correspondents for French newspapers in American cities, and of course the greatly increased transatlantic travel.

It was during this period that the "American in Paris "came into existence. American businessmen, tourists, diplomats, artists, writers, adventurers, land promoters, and political agitators became familiar figures in the streets, salons, and political meetings of Paris. A number also attempted to establish themselves in various French cities as importers, exporters, or speculators.

There were also famous names among these Americans. John Paul Jones returned to France in 1784 and again in 1790 after service in the navy of Catherine the Great. The poet Joel Barlow arrived in 1788, the painter John Trumbull in 1786, and in the same year, the architect Charles Bullfinch. The already known and admired Thomas Paine travelled to Paris in 1787. At least forty-three different editions of his various works were published in France, including no less than eleven of his *Rights of Man*.

Aside from Franklin, the most important American founding father to visit France after the Revolutionary War was Thomas Jefferson. Unlike Franklin, Jefferson did not seek the limelight. Consequently, in the political debates which so frequently cited American examples, Jefferson was seldom mentioned. Much more of a nationalist than the cosmopolitan Franklin, he was reserved in his acceptance of French ways, and his friendships in Paris, though they were many, were discriminating. He could never become a public hero like Franklin.[17]

Whereas Franklin's efforts had been mainly directed toward creating in the French mind a favorable picture of America, Jefferson's were directed towards creating an accurate one. He was much disturbed by the reports of political chaos in the United States being spread in Europe by the English press, and he attempted to refute them by writing articles in the pro-American *Gazette de Leyde* and other European newspapers.[18]

One of the most important contributions of these Americans in Paris, and of their French friends, was to make available to the French public the best products of American thought and to provide for the first time a valid documentation for the French image of America.

The activity of American diplomats and of French collaborators like Lafayette in disseminating pro-American views was stimulated by the fact that from 1783 on there appeared in France an important current of anti-Americanism. It is true that the government, both royal and Revolutionary, remained officially friendly, and that a large majority of the intellectuals and liberal politicians were strongly pro-American and that the people had not lost the fraternal affection aroused by Franklin and the war. Nevertheless there was a considerable minority who, without being aggressively hostile, were pessimistic about the success of the new nation, took pleasure in debunking the American dream, and received news of American difficulties and failures with something approaching satisfaction. The division of opinion was a conflict of political and economic interests on which the United States had a very real bearing. As one observer remarked in 1786:

---

17 Thomas Jefferson, J. P. Boyd, ed.., *The Papers of Thomas Jefferson* (Princeton: Princeton University Press, 1950), III, p. 568-570

18 Jefferson to Abigail Adams, November 20, 1785

"Since the revolution which assured the sovereignty of the United States, European observers have painted of conditions there pictures which are sometimes enthusiastic and sometimes lamentable. The different colors under which the United States has been represented are the product of a great diversity of opinions, and we may affirm without fear of contradiction that party spirit, prejudice, and politics have invented three-quarters of the descriptions."[19]

The principle source of news about the United States came from the English press, which was quite understandably unfavorable to its former colonies, but in many cases it was the only source of American information that the French press could obtain. So as examples, the French newspapers printed reports of the American population having been decreased because of the war, that the importation of slaves had increased, that indentured servants were actually "white slaves", and that Americans were failing to meet their obligations to British creditors.

Whatever the sources of these reports, they were welcomed by conservatives and royalists who, reacting against the idealization of America as the triumph of liberalism, democracy, and republicanism were anxious to find evidence of the failure of these principles. Lafayette found such sentiments prevalent in European courts, which were causing a decline in America's reputation "which delights her enemies, harms her interests even with her friends, and provides the opponents of liberty with anti-republican arguments."[20]

To the French liberals, the danger was even greater, for it threatened to produce an attitude of cynicism and disillusion toward America and the political ideals she represented. There were ample signs of such an attitude. The Abbe Mably, in his influential *Observations surle* gouvernement et les des Etats-Unis printed in 1784 expressed serious doubts about the success of the American

---

19 Journal Politique de Bruxelles, August, 12, 1786

20 Lafayette to Jefferson, Sept. 4, 1785

republics. He had little faith in the political wisdom of the common man, and he warned that democracy, however good it might be in principle, when unmodified as in the United States by aristocratic institutions, was dangerous and impractical. Francois Soules, in his *Historie des troubles de l'Ameriqueanglaise* derided the writers who believed that all the inhabitants of the United States were virtuous men acting on noble principles. "They do not realize that in America the wise are few indeed in comparison with the ignorant, the selfish, and those men who blindly allow themselves to be led – those who in the kingdoms of Europe are known as the people."[21]

Not all anti-Americanism was political in nature. Some arose from economic causes. Charles Graviercomte de Vergennes (Vergennes), the French foreign minister in making the decision in 1778 to support the United States against England, had argued that American independence would inflict irreparable losses on English trade and would considerably increase American trade with France. After the Treaty of Paris ending the war was signed in 1793, the French expected that the profitable trade between England and America, would now become trade between America and France for three reasons – American enmity towards England, American gratitude towards France, and England's restrictive trade policy. Unfortunately for the French however by 1789, British exports had risen to prewar levels even over the imports from America. On the other hand, French exports to America, though greater than before the war, remained far below English exports. Most of the problems between the two countries were on the French side. Americans were discouraged from shipping their products to France by the tobacco monopoly of the Fermegenerale (Farmers General) an organization that outsourced customs, excise, and indirect taxes on behalf of the king, by the strangling mass of red tape, by excessive duties on certain items which delayed unloading of many products, and by lack of demand for a number of important American products. Also, French exporters attempted to dump shoddy merchandise into the

---

21 Francois Soules, *Historire des troubles de l'Ameriqueanglaise* (1787), IV, p. 263-264

United States which went unsold or sold at a loss. The result was that American confidence in French manufactures and French interest in American markets was destroyed. More serious was the fact that Americans were used to English goods and French manufactures would not modify their products to fit the demands of the American market. On the financial side, the French were unwilling to grant the long terms of credit that Americans were used to receiving from the English. There were also problems caused by the Americans. First some debts contracted by Americans in France were not honored and many French companies who did business with American companies suffered losses because of American bankruptcies. Finally, there was the matter of the American public debt. The United States still owed the French volunteer officers a large amount of back pay, plus interest, a neglected obligation which Jefferson warned "would give birth to new imputations, and a relapse of credit."[22] In addition, of course was the national foreign debt, the repayment of which seemed very uncertain.

Putting all these circumstances together, the French believed that: the Americans had a low standard of business ethics and that the economic position of the United States was very shaky, and secondly there was the idea that the Americans did not feel any gratitude for the aid they were given during the war and that at heart, they were still attached to England.

Much of the contention surrounding trade centered on the West Indies. In 1784, the colonial planters persuaded the French government to issue an arret[23] opening seven West Indian ports into which foreign traders would be permitted to import from the United States and other nations certain products, mainly salt beef, salt fish, and wheat and to export molasses, rum, and goods of French origin. The decree produced a storm of protests among French shippers, who previously had a monopoly on this considerably profitable

---

22 "Jefferson's Report on Conversations with Vergennes, "Jefferson Papers, op. cit. IX, 139-145

23 A judicial decision

trade, causing ill feeling on the part of French merchants towards American and English shippers.

There were attempts to preserve good relations between the United States and France so that there could be mutually profitable trade between the countries. As an example, Jefferson attempted to modify the control of the Farmers General over tobacco, which would have been the main import crop from the United States to France. In 1787, Nicholas Bergasse, a Parisian lawyer, founded the Societe Gallo-Americiane in 1787 to promote commercial relations between the two countries and to foster mutual understanding and friendship. These friendly efforts did bring about some action on the part of the French government, but it is doubtful that they had much effect on the opinions of French businessmen.

The situation became even worse by the activities of American land companies who had been selling American frontier land in Paris since 1788. The social chaos of the French Revolution boosted the sales greatly. First because it was an opportunity to buy vast amounts of land at very cheap prices and secondly, it looked to be a safe investment, especially to frightened aristocrats in search of asylum. The most outrageous of these land schemes was the one organized by the Scioto Company in August 1789, one month after the fall of the Bastille. In an atmosphere of violence, uncertainty, and insecurity, the company's salesmen painted a glowing picture of their products that it seemed to many Frenchmen to be a solution to their fears and problems. During the summer of 1790, about one thousand French emigrants left their country for the state of Ohio, only to find that the land that they purchased was not theirs since the Scioto Company did not own the land, but rather only had an option on it. Additionally, the journey to these lands in Ohio was extremely arduous, there was an Indian war in the same area, there was no provisions (which had been guaranteed), and finally, that the Scioto Company was on the verge of bankruptcy.[24]

---

24 T. T. Belote, *The Scioto Speculation and the French Settlement at Gallipolis* (New York: B. Franklin, 1971

Many of the settlers scattered to various American cities, but most returned to France. The tragic affair received a great deal of attention, especially in the newspapers, and the reaction in France was political. Since those who left were aristocrats the revolutionists interpreted their actions as a lack of faith in the new order. The aristocrats understandably had little good to say of the United States. They felt, with some justification that they had been swindled and their resentment became generalized into extreme anti-Americanism. One of them described the United States thus: "The inhabitant bears on his brow the mark of poverty and dishonor; religion and marriage are unknown; bad food and bad drink; the only thing that is good is the wood. Winter lasts six months there, and it is very cold; the heat too is excessive, and the days are very short in all seasons."[25]

This strong anti-democratic and anti-republican bias was also evident in the French diplomatic corps. In August 1787, the French Ministry of Foreign Affairs sent the following communication to its Charge d'Affaires in America, Louis-Guillaume Otto:

> It appears, sir that in all the American provinces there is more or less tendency toward democracy that in many this extreme form of government will finally prevail. The result will be that the confederation will have little stability and that by degrees the different states will subsist in perfect independence of each other. This revolution will not be regretted by us. We have never pretended to make of America a useful ally; we have had no other object than to deprive Great Britain of that vast continent. Therefore we can regard with indifference both the movements which agitate certain provinces and the fermentation which prevails in Congress.[26]

Also in 1787, as American delegates met in Philadelphia to covert an impotent confederation into the world's first federated republic by creating a Constitution, the first French ambassador to

---

25 D'Allemagne, *Nouvelles du Scioto*, (Paris, 1790)

26 George Bancroft, *History of the Formation of the Constitution* (New York: D. Appleton, 1882), p. 438

the United Stated, Conrad Alexandre Gerard de Rayneval met with Benjamin Franklin, Silas Deane, and Arthur Lee to sign the Treaty of Alliance with the United States, However according to Talleyrand, he had an ulterior motive – to prevent agreement on the creation of the American Constitution:

> The French ambassador had instructions to block the enterprise. This same ally that had sacrificed so much to separate the American states from England, wanted to keep them disunited and separated from each other. [France] wanted to condemn them to a long and difficult infancy to keep them weak, without the means to govern or defend themselves effectively. The ambassador obeyed his instructions to the best of his ability by opposing passage of the Constitution during the convention [in Philadelphia] and in each state legislature during the subsequent ratification proceedings. Although his efforts failed to block passage, they did help sow the seeds of anti federalism that would sap the United States strength for generations.[27]

It is against this minority current of anti-Americanism that the American Dream appears in its true perspective. It was the defense as well as the affirmation of a certain ideological and political position. As such, it constituted an important element in the current of ideas flowing toward the French Revolution. It was essentially the belief that certain key doctrines of the century were achieving their first realization in the United States. The greater the faith in these doctrines, the greater was the tendency to exaggerate their success in America, and thus to fashion an idealized image of American life. It was a projection of French aspirations upon a scene which was both accommodating and distant enough to blur the inconsistencies and contradictions.

But the supreme proof of the equality of opportunity under the American system was again Benjamin Franklin because his example proved that in a free nation any man, no matter what his origin,

---

27   Michael Poniatowski, *Talleyrand aux Etats-Unis, 1794-1796* (Paris: Presses de la Cite, 1967), p. 350

could reach the top, and therefore that society could draw its leaders from all classes. Franklin's lifelong friend, Jean Baptiste Le Roy wrote in 1790 . . . . In Paris, that great man (Franklin), under the *ancien regime*, would have remained in obscurity; for how could one have put to use the son of a candle maker? Or even if his scientific genius could have broken down the barriers erected by his inferior social position, he would have remained at most a member of some academy.[28]

The counter-revolution of Thermidor[29] marked the end of the American Dream in France. At this point, there became a clear line between the Emigres who lived in the United States and the remainder of the French people. In 1788, the major first hand opinion of the United States came from those involved in the Scioto disaster. But with the beginning of the revolution in 1789, a great many Frenchmen were forced to take refuge in foreign lands. They streamed out of France in two waves: the first, the "Voluntary Emigration" starting in the summer of 1789 was composed of royalists frightened by the storming of the Bastille; the second, the "Forced Emigration" beginning in late 1971 to mid-1794 was the flight of those who had collaborated in the early stages of the Revolution, who were literally fleeing for their lives. The majority of these refugees remained in Europe, usually in England and Germany, but a considerable number – estimated between 10,000 and 25,000 – crossed the Atlantic.[30]

Most of the second wave of Émigrés who came to America had left France for the practical purpose of saving their lives, and to that end were forced by economic necessity to integrate themselves into

---

28 Claude Fauchet, *Elogecivique de Benjamin Franklin* (Paris, 1790, first edition), p. 45

29 Thermidor refers to the coup of July 27, 1794 in which the French Committee of Public Safety led by Maximilen Robespierre was terminated and replaced by the Directory which instituted more conservative policies aimed at stabilizing the revolutionary government.

30 F. S. Childs, *French Refugee Life in the United States, 1790-1800* (Baltimore: Johns Hopkins University Press, 1940), p. 9-10

American life in order to make a living. It might have been expected that these men and women would arrive with a favorable disposition toward their new home since Pro-Americanism was still dominant in France. The opposite however became the case, since these emigrants soon lost whatever favorable predispositions they may have had and quickly conceived, in most cases, an extreme aversion to all things American. The Duke de La Rochefoucauld-Liancourt noted in his diary soon after his arrival in 1794, "All the French I have met so far have little liking for America and less still for Americans."[31] This widespread and extreme reaction against American life was the central factor in the new attitudes and ideas generated by the Emigration into the United States.

While not all Emigres developed a poor opinion of the United States after living in America, for most however, the American Dream was dead. This view was shared by Charles Maurice de Talleyrand-Perigord (Talleyrand), who would later become France's foreign minister. Writing to Mme de Stael,[32] "If I have to stay in this country a year I shall die."[33]

It would be natural to suppose that the Dream died because these Emigres witnessed the reality of living in the United States, but there was a more relevant reason – that the Dream became unnecessary. It had been created to prove that certain ideals such as political and civic liberty were universally true. However when the French Revolution began, those who believed in this ideals had their own example, and therefore did not need the experience of America. There was also over idealization of America, exemplified by such writers as Hector St. Jean de Crevecoeur (Crevecoeur), a naturalized American citizen who had lived in America since the French and Indian War and wrote an extremely popular book

---

31 Francois Alexandre Frederic, Duc de La Rochefoucauld-Liancourt, *Journal de voyage enAmerique et d'un sejour a Philadephie*, ed. J. Marchand (Baltimore, 1940), p. 62

32 A French writer who fled France during the Revolution and who later became an enemy of Napolean.

33 G. Lacour-Gayet, *Talleyrand* (Paris, 1928-1931), p. 199

about the country entitled, *Lettres d'un cultivateur American*[34] which portrayed American society as characterized by the principles of equal opportunity and self-determination. Filippo Mazzei, an Italian visitor who was a close friend of Thomas Jefferson's and who was also an unofficial roving ambassador in Europe of American ideals and institutions cautioned against Crevecoeur's vision of America in his book, *Recherches*, "I ought to warn the readers of the *Lettres d'un cultivateur American* to be careful not to imagine that the manners and customs described in that book are general in America. . . . I have been very much surprised to learn that many people have conceived the most chimerical notions from the reading of this book. . . My intention is not to discourage Europeans who would like to become American citizens, but only to save them from regretting too late that they have done so."[35]

American life, whether in Philadelphia or on the frontier was far removed from the existence the Emigres had known in France. They discovered that Americans in their traditions, values, and thinking were fundamentally different from themselves. They had come to an alien, not a fraternal land. This feeling of depaysement[36], when added to all the other sufferings, intensified an awakened affection for their lost homeland and produced in these men a deep and brooding nostalgia. They were sick with longing for France, for French ways and for French speech. This was something genuinely new in this century, a true *amorpatriae* – an attachment not to one's class, nor one's friends, but to the very soil of France. One homesick Frenchman put it this way in a letter, "Far from my native land, which is still dear to me, and from the friends of my youth, plunged in a sort of constant unhappiness, my imagination delights in the memory of former affections and it is not without effort that I fix my attention on things alien to the emotions which fill my heart."[37]

34 Letters from an American Farmer

35 Filippo Mazzei, *Recherches*, iv, 1788, p. 98-100

36 The feeling that comes from not being in one's home country.

37 Antoine Jay, "Correspondance inedited d'un Francis qui a reside dans les Etats-Unis, depuisl'annee 1795 jusqu'em, 1803" *Bibliothequeamericaine* (Paris, 1807),

Inevitably, this new patriotism worked against any affection or sympathy for a foreign soil.

The French in America also began to realize that while they found it difficult to adapt to American life, Northern Europeans found it to be relatively easy because of the similarity of political and ethical traditions. Constantin Francois de Chasseboeuf, comte de Volney (Volney) a French nobleman and historian said of this situation, "the French encounter obstacles in the differences of language, laws, customs, manners and even taste. . . .It cannot be denied . . . that there exists between the two people a conflict of customs and social forms which makes any close union very difficult."[38] Talleyrand put it in stronger terms, "I have not found a single Englishman who did not feel at home among Americans, and not a single Frenchman who did not feel a stranger."[39] This idea that Americans were closer to Great Britain than France pervaded the thinking of many Frenchmen who commented on the favoritism of the United States towards England in spite of the recent war. That American values and mores were much closer to those of England than those of France. Ferdinand Marie Bayard (Bayard), a French writer and traveler in the United States claimed that "All the errors and vices of England have flooded the cities of America."[40] The French journalist, Antoine Jay condemned American subservience to the dictates of English tastes and fashion, the perverse American admiration for Shakespeare, and in particular the production of plays written in another land for another audience which neither portrayed American manners nor presented ideas and sentiments adapted to American society. To Talleyrand, this imposition of English customs and patterns of thought on the United States explained why the two

---

no.4, p. 1-2

38 Constantin, Comte de Volney, *Tableau du climat et du sol des Etats-Unis de l'Amerique* (Paris, 1803), p. xiii

39 Talleyrand, " Memoire sur la relations commerciales des Etats-Unis," *Memorires de l'Institut des Sciences etArts,Sciences Morales et Politiques*, II, an VII, p. 92

40 Ferdinand Marie Bayard, Voyage dansl'interieur des Etats-Unis pendant l'ete de 1791 (Paris, an VI), p. 32

peoples responded to reason rather than emotion, why they were the only modern nations without "society," and why both were essentially incompatible to the French.

Thus the new sense of nationalism produced the belief that an unbridgeable chasm divided the Frenchman and the American that each must inevitably remain a stranger in the other's land. The very fact that the new republic, so long spiritually and economically dependent on the European motherland was now turning its face westward

It was obvious to every Émigré that the United States was in the midst of a period of great economic expansion. Antoine Jay wrote, "The annals of nations offer us no spectacle more extraordinary and imposing than the rapid expansion of the United States in population and power."[41] Talleyrand was particularly impressed by the rapid westward movement of the frontier and the miraculous rise of the farms and towns in areas where a few years before had been wilderness. Writing to Mme. De Stael, he said that America was "the best place in the world to make money fast."[42] When Talleyrand sneered that in America "money is the universal God," he did not mean that he condemned Americas for sacrificing ethical principles to economic profits. What he despised was a nation where "the quantity of money a man possesses is the only means of distinction," where wealth outweighed birth, breeding, and intellectual or artistic achievement, where men had no interest in any activity that did not produce a tangible return, and where taste and refinement were disesteemed. This was the inevitable reaction of men who were still aristocrats by instinct and already romantics without knowing the name. "For as old Europeans," Talleyrand complained, "there is something gauche about the way Americans spend their money. I admit that our own extravagance is often foolish and frivolous, but American extravagance is such that it only seems to prove that no

---

41 Antoine Jay, "Correspondance," no. 4, p. 2

42 H. Huthe and W. J. Pugh, *Talleyrand in America as a Financial Promoter, 1794-1796* (Washington: U.S. Govt. Printing Office, 1942), p. 145

delicacy in the art of living, even in the art of living foolishly, has yet penetrated the American character."[43] Love of money according to the Emigres was at the root of the American evil.

The main force that kept alive any good will between the two nations was the hope for economic and military support from across the Atlantic against the power of England. As an example the *Decade philosophique,* the first literary and intellectual periodical to emerge after the French Revolution declared in an article entitled *Moniteuruniversel* in 1794, "Americans are united with the French not only by bonds of gratitude but even more by their love of liberty." The article went on to say that is was the tangible expressions of gratitude that the writer was interested in such as American shipments of wheat and the chances of an armed alliance.[44] Additionally, reports were printed frequently of American celebrations in honor of French military victories and the news of General "Mad" Anthony Wayne's victory against the combined force of American Indian and British troops at the Battle of Fallen Timbers, which was optimistically hailed as the outbreak of a new American war against the England. Such expectations found expression in the enthusiastic reception given James Monroe by the French government in August 1794 and the presentation to Congress of a Tricolor in return for Monroe's gift of an American flag.

French opinion of the United States must also include those royalist Emigres living not in the new nation, but rather in other European countries. These aristocrats blamed the Americans for all the catastrophes they had suffered in their native land. Lafayette wrote Washington that the hatred of the aristocrat party for America dated from the beginning of the French Revolution.[45] Joseph de Maistre, a French philosopher, writer, and lawyer saw the monarchy as a divinely sanctioned institution and the only stable form of government in attacking the principle of democratic republicanism

---

43 Talleyrand, *Memoires, lettres, et papiers secrets,* ed. J. Garcia (Paris, 1891), p. 61

44 Moniteur universal, Decade philosophique, Dec. 1 & 22, 1794

45 Lafayette, *Memoires, correspondence, et manuscrits* (Paris, 1837-1838), iv, p. 436

wrote in 1797, "People give the example of America. I know nothing so exasperating as the praises bestowed on that babe in swaddling clothes; wait till it grows up."[46] He also made the point that traditions and circumstances were so different between France and the United States that it was impossible to draw any analogies in comparing them. Going further, Charles Pictet, a Swiss expressed the greatest admiration for the fact that the American Revolution avoided any violent disruption in its social structure, but attributed this success to special circumstance in America: long established traditions of liberty and self-government, the strength of religion in the United States, the continuity of leadership, the predominantly agricultural population, and finally, the deep rooted American sense of civic responsibility.[47]

On July 14, 1789, the French people who had lived for centuries under autocratic rule stormed through Paris and attacked the Bastille, the hated symbol of autocratic rule in France.. The impetus for this action was the signing of a document much like the American Constitution by the National Assembly, which included the Rights of Man, a clause which was signed by the king ending absolute monarchy in France. After three years of chaos, the National Assembly voted itself out of existence. The National Assembly which replaced it, abolished the French royalty and declared France a republic like the United States. The government at this point was under the control of the Girondin[48] leader, Jacques Pierre Brissot, a journalist who had no experience in government administration. To solve the two most pressing problems facing the nation – starvation and anarchy, Brissot sent hungry French mobs to topple other kings as they had toppled their own. "We will not be satisfied until Europe – all Europe – is aflame, France had been called to lead a gigantic revolution [and a] worldwide uprising to liberate the oppressed

---

46 Joseph de Maistre, *Considerations sur la France* (London, 1797), p.65

47 Durand Echeverria, Mirage in the West, p. 207-223

48 The Girondins were a party of bourgeois merchants from the Gironde region of Southwestern France who favored a peaceful revolution to replace absolute monarchy with a constitutional monarchy.

peoples of the world. All Europe, as far as Moscow will be Gallicized, communized, and Jacobinized."[49]

Brissot revived the centuries old French policy of self-enrichment from conquest and plunder by converting the nation's hunger into a virtual crusade that spread across Europe piling up one military victory after another. To the delight of Brissot and the Girondin's, profits from foreign plunder poured into the French treasury. As they had done in France, French revolutionaries seized assets of royals, aristocrats, and churches in every conquered land.

Far from bankrupting France as the American revolutionary war had done, the French Revolution resolved the nation's immediate fiscal crisis. Foreign plunder replenished the French treasury and rebuilt the nation's military and naval strength. The plunder did little to relieve French agriculture or ease famine however because of a drought that decimated the crop yields in southern France, and the peasants who would have tended the crops in northern France were engaged in foreign wars.

Brissot's solution to the problem was to absorb the United States into the French sphere of influence. He would convert the United States into a source of foodstuffs to end the famine in France, and additionally America would supply raw materials for French manufactures for conversion into finished goods for the American market. Thomas Jefferson had himself proposed "mutual naturalization" of French and American merchants to allow them to buy and sell duty-free in both countries as if they were citizens of each.

Brissot knew that Americans were deeply sympathetic to the French Revolution and that many echoed Jefferson's calls for closer economic ties with France. He conceived the idea of sending the King and the royal family – then in prison facing death – into exile in America as a gesture of friendship. Thomas Paine had pleaded

---

49 Henry Ammon, *The Genet Mission* (New York: W. W. Norton & Company, 1973), p. 20

that "France has today but one friend: the American Republic. Do not give the United States the sorrow . . . of witnessing the death upon the scaffold of a man who has aided my American brethren in breaking the fetters of English despotism."[50] Brissot also knew that Americans were very appreciative of Louis XVI's support of their revolution and would certainly not look favorably on his execution.

On January 21, 1793, the French Convention ignored Paine and Brissot and set the king to the guillotine for "conspiring with foreigners . . . to deprive the nation of liberty."[51] And ten days later, France declared war on England, subsequently Spain declared war on France.

Besieged on all sides and still facing a famine from a year long drought, the French called on their American ally (under the Franco-American Treaty of 1788) to attack British and Spanish colonies in North America which would force Britain to open a second front thereby relaxing its blockade of French ports. The French strategy was offensive as well as defensive. French military and naval forces in the French West Indies planned to sail to the American mainland, link up with American troops, and invade British Canada and Spanish held Florida and Louisiana. Ultimately Franco-American forces would overrun the entire hemisphere and seize the Spanish gold and silver mines of Mexico and Peru.

At this time England and Spain were allied by treaty after almost going to war over the Nootka Sound controversy.[52] Also at this time, the British controlled the forts in the American Northwest and were encouraging the Indians to hold the Ohio River.[53] The British had for several years been gathering information on the attitude of the northwestern settlers toward possible English control of the

50 Meade Minnigerode, *Jefferson, Friend of France* (New York: G. P. Putnam & Sons, 1928) p. 133

51 *Le Petit Robert des NomsPropres* (Paris: Dictionnaries Le Robert, 1999), p. 1253

52 A dispute over control of navigation and trade in the president day Canadian province of British Columbia

53 Before the Battle of Fallen Timbers.

area. On April 17, 1790, the Lords of the Privy Council for Trade wrote to Lord Grenville, the Secretary of State for Home Affairs, that Vermont and the western settlements should be given a liberal policy of commercial concession and "in a commercial view it will be for the Benefit of this Country to prevent Vermont and Kentucky and all the other settlements now forming in the interior parts of the great Continent of North America, from becoming dependent on the Government of the United States, or on that of any other Foreign Country, and to preserve them on the contrary in a State of Independence, and to induce them to form Treaties of Commerce and Friendship with Great Britain."[54] Spain was also involved in looking after their areas of interest in America. In Kentucky and Tennessee, they supported the Creeks, Cherokees, and other Indians in the Gulf region against any American advance into their territories and at the same time denying to the settlers of these regions the right to navigate the Mississippi with their aim to secure the independence of Kentucky and Tennessee under Spanish protection. Brissot realized the discontent of the western Americans over the closure of the Mississippi by the Spanish, "They are determined to open it by good will or by force; and it would not be in the power of Congress to moderate their ardor. Men who have shook off the yoke of Great Britain, and who are masters of the Ohio and the Mississippi, cannot conceive that the insolence of a handful of Spaniards can think of shutting rivers and seas against a hundred thousand free Americans. The slightest quarrel will be sufficient to throw them into a flame; and if ever the Americans shall March towards New Orleans, it will infallibly fall into their hands."[55]

Edmond-Charles Genet, the new ambassador to the United States, arrived in Charleston South Carolina on April 8, 1793 ostensibly to promote support for France's wars with Spain and Britain beginning with the announcement that France was granting duty free status to all American goods exported to that country. His actual goals were more dramatic, Genet was sent to the United States

---

54 *Report on Canadian Archives*, 1890, p. 132

55 Jacques Pierre Brissot, *Nouveau Voyage dans les Etats-Unis* (Paris, 1791)

with a secret mission to foment a revolution in the American Spanish colonies by forming a connection with the American frontiersmen and then seize Louisiana, Florida, and Canada, in much the same way that the French armies swept across Europe in the early days of the Revolution. In this case France reckoned upon the active support or the connivance of the American people, and particularly the irate Kentuckians to aid her in repelling the Spanish from the approaches to the Mississippi, and perhaps from both North and South America.

To aid in reaching his objective, Genet attempted to enlist Thomas Jefferson. If the Secretary of State and leader of the Democratic party could be actively enlisted in the project, to Genet its success would be certain. Initially, Genet believed that Jefferson was in agreement with the French plan because if the United States went to war with Spain, French assistance would be valuable, however Jefferson came to believe that Genet wished to force the United States into a war with Spain. Finally, even though Jefferson as a Democrat was a supporter of France as opposed to the Federalist support of Great Britain, Genet's actions over the *Little Democrat*[56] soon compelled Jefferson to abandon him, declaring "his conduct is indefensible by the most furious Jacobin. I only wish our countrymen may distinguish between him and his nation."[57]

After the *Little Democrat* affair, and Genet's continuing actions against the British, President Washington sent Genet an 8000 word letter of complaint. When Genet did not cease in sending out privateers, both Hamilton and Jefferson urged his recall as ambassador by France. The Jacobins having taken power in France by January 1794 sent an arrest notice to the United States asking

---

56 When Genet arrived in the United States, he began to issue privateering commissions. These commissions authorized the bearers, regardless of their country of origin, to seize British merchant ships and their cargoes for personal profit with the approval of the French government. Jefferson informed him that the United States considered the outfitting of French privateers in American ports to be a violation of the U. S. policy of neutrality. Genet ignored the warning and outfitted the *Little Democrat*, which set sail to attack British shipping.

57 Jefferson to James Monroe, Sept. 12, 1793

that Genet be sent back to France. Genet, knowing that he would be likely be sent to the guillotine, asked Washington for asylum, which was granted thanks to Alexander Hamilton, his fiercest opponent in Washington's cabinet.

Chapter 2

President Washington and the International Situation

In his annual address to Congress in 1790, President Washington called attention to the disturbing situation in Europe and the necessity for circumspection on the part of the United States.[1] At the beginning of 1791, France registered a complaint about certain duties imposed by the United States, which caused a discussion in the American government as to the interpretation of the Treaty of Commerce promulgated between the United States and France in 1778, at this point however there no serious difficulties between the two countries until the general European war between France and other European nations, most notably, Great Britain, brought on by the French Revolution.

A strict fulfillment of our treaty obligations would have drawn the United States into this war as an ally of France. The major question discussed in Washington's cabinet about the war and America's place in it was whether the treaties signed with Louis XVI were still valid, taking into consideration the change in government in France, brought about by the revolution. The consensus was that the agreement was still in force. According to the eleventh article of the treaty of alliance the United States guaranteed "to his Most Christian Majesty the present possessions of the Crown of France in

---

1 State Papers and Publick Documents of the United States [Edited by T. B. Wait.] Third Edition., vol. 1,, Boston, 1819, p.18

34

America, as well as those which it may acquire by the future treaty of peace. "This referred especially to the French West Indies and to have complied with the treaty would have involved the United States in the defense of these islands against English attacks. In view of the exhausted military condition of the United States at this time, slowly recovering from the strain of the War of Independence and loaded with debt, to have embarked on another war would have been suicidal, so the decision was made that the United States should practice strict neutrality. In February, 1793, after the execution of King Louis XVI, the war spread across Europe involving not only France and Great Britain, but also Spain and Holland.

In order to assess the opinions of his cabinet, President Washington asked them a series of questions relating to the situation and also gained their approval on two important measures; first that neutrality should be proclaimed and that the Republic of France should be recognized and that a French minister should be received. While Jefferson agreed with the Federalists that neutrality was the best course, he believed that there was no need to make a Proclamation of Neutrality either immediately or officially. The United States could declare its neutrality for a price, his idea, "Why not stall and make countries bid for [American] neutrality?"[2] In response, Hamilton declared that American neutrality was not negotiable. On April 22, 1793, Washington issued his proclamation, in which he declared that the United States will "pursue a conduct friendly and impartial toward the belligerent powers." That American citizens engaged in contraband trade will not be protected by the government against punishment or forfeiture, and that the United States will prosecute all persons who violate the law of nations. It was agreed that the word "neutrality "should be omitted from the text of the proclamation.[3] Although the proclamation was approved by both the Senate and the House of Representatives, it was not announced until more than a year later on June 4, 1794. The proclamation was not popular with the American people, probably because they still were

2 Ron Chernow, *Alexander Hamilton* (New York: Penguin, 2004), p. 435

3 *Ibid.* p. 44

extremely favorable towards the French who had been so instrumental in America winning its revolution against Great Britain. However, the American people had the opportunity to see both sides of the issue because of the Pacificus-Helvidius debates between Alexander Hamilton and James Madison. Hamilton (Pacificus) wrote a letter in the *Gazette of the United States,* printed in Philadelphia on June 29, 1793 supporting Washington's Proclamation. In the Pacificus letters, Hamilton argued that the president's power to make such a proclamation issues from a general grant of executive power in Article II of the Constitution which (as he outlined it) includes conducting foreign relations; from the president's primary responsibility in the formation of treaties; and from the power of the execution of the laws, of which treaties form a part. He pointed out in Pacificus that the first sentence of Article II of the Constitution which declares that "the executive power shall be vested in a President," was meant as a general grant of power, not merely a designation of office, despite the enumeration of executive powers in other sections of Article II, and that moreover this general grant leaves the full range of executive powers to be discovered by interpreting it "in conformity to other parts [of] the constitution and to the principles of free government."[4] This made the decree constitutional, for while Congress has the sole right to declare war, it is "the duty of the executive to preserve peace till war is declared."[5]

Normally in this situation, the rebuttal to an argument by the leader of one faction (in this case Alexander Hamilton as the leader of the Federalists) would be answered by the leader of the group holding an opposite viewpoint (Thomas Jefferson as the Republican leader), but Jefferson asked Madison as the Republican leader in the Senate to reply to Hamilton, as Jefferson at first backed the Proclamation and then changed his mind when he came to the conclusion that Hamilton was using the neutrality issue to extend the area of executive control of foreign affairs. In his letter to Madison, Jefferson stated "Nobody answers him, & his doctrine will therefore

4   Pacificus no. 1, June 29, 1793

5   *Ibid.*

be taken for confessed, For God's sake, my dear Sir, take up your pen, select the most striking heresies, and cut him to pieces in the face of the public. There is nobody else who can & will enter the lists with him."[6]

In reply to Hamilton, Madison, writing as Helvidius claimed that Hamilton's reading of executive power introduced "new principles and new constructions" into the Constitution that were intended to remove the "landmarks of power." It was the violation of the Constitution issuing from the introduction of these "new principle and constructions" that most concerned Madison as well as Jefferson, who saw it as in effect undermining the very sanctity of the constitutional document. Hamilton, Madison believed, was arguing that the direction of foreign policy was essentially an executive function, whereas he, Madison was arguing that the direction of foreign policy was essentially a legislative function by virtue of the Senate's treaty-making and war powers.[7] The Republicans also argued that the Proclamation would violate America's defensive alliance with France. In rebuttal, Hamilton pointed out that the treaty was a defensive alliance and did not apply to offensive wars, "and it was France that had declared war upon other European powers," not the other way around.[8]

The proclamation emphasized that the United States would act in an "impartial" manner towards England and France. Many American friends of France in the United States believed that a neutrality which leaned towards France would have been more appropriate. Also both Jefferson and Madison were disturbed by Washington's enhancing the power of the executive by taking upon himself the authority to issue the proclamation. They believed that as Congress had the power to issue a declaration of war, it should also have the power to issue a declaration of neutrality. Their arguments however were to no avail, the Pacificus-Helvidius debate did not

6   Jefferson to Madison, July 7, 1793

7   Helvidius no.4, September 14, 1793

8   Ron Chernow, *Alexander Hamilton*, p. 442

dissuade Washington from following Hamilton's interpretation of the powers of the president.[9] The debates did however clarify the constitutional principle that the direction of foreign policy is essentially an executive function in spite of Madison's strict constructionist viewpoint which demanded that Congress, not the president, had full authority over all foreign affairs except those specified in the Constitution. As a result of his disagreement with the Proclamation of Neutrality, Jefferson eventually resigned his position as Secretary of State.

The differences between the ideas of Hamilton and the Federalists on the one hand and those of Jefferson and Madison as Democratic Republicans on the other, began to crystallize in the first session of Congress. James Madison called for discrimination against British ships and outlined a plan to free the new nation from British dominance of the carrying trade, credit facilities, and heavy dependence on imports from England.

New England's representatives in Congress dismissed the Madison proposal as unrealistic, even though at this early stage, they were not wholly in favor of England over France, they simply believed that his ideas were too impractical. Falling back on their experience as merchants and shippers, they knew that it would be too costly to engage England in economic warfare. Additionally, they were dependent on British credit and that only England produced the manufactured goods that they imported, even though they realized that the United States would have to withstand British restrictions on their trade. The Federalists realistically believed that Britain and France as major powers would regulate trade to their own advantage, ignoring the wishes of a weaker nation. It was simply business, Britain and France were competing and the United States was in the middle. American merchants, whose daily transactions aimed at profit, could hardly find this competition in any way against the very nature of life. It was just part of the ups and downs of the market.

---

9   Reginald Horsman, *The Diplomacy of the New Republic, 1776-1815* (Arlington Heights, Illinois: Harlan Davidson, Inc., 1985), p. 50

The leader of the Federalist opposition to Madison at this time was Fisher Ames, a Congressman from Massachusetts. Madison's proposal that we should not deal with nations that we have no treaties with, e.g. Great Britain, and therefore become closer to France, produced the following from Ames, that he was "strongly opposed to being led by the principle of gratitude in matters relative to the public weal. "Referring to the treaty with France, Ames laid down the rule that the obligation incurred, "never required more than what its terms stipulated for; therefore on matters of commerce and revenue; interest ought to be predominately principle."[10] Theodore Sedgwick, a senator from Massachusetts, speaking out on Madison's idea of placing high duties against British ships in order to favor France declared the measure to be "of very great impropriety." His hostility erupted into a denunciatory series of questions: "Who are concerned in the carrying trade? We are declaring against one country in favor of another; for what purpose? Do gentlemen expect that France will aid our carrying trade? . . . .It is a useless declaration, an important measure of passion, not dictated by the understanding . . . .?"[11]

The situation became very much one of New England vs. James Madison. Fisher Ames epitomized the strengths and weaknesses of the New England coterie. On the one hand, he had a grudging admiration for Madison as "a man of sense, reading, address, and integrity"; yet, on the other hand, he distrusted Madison because he found him "Very much Frenchified in his politics. "And most tellingly, "Madison, he concluded, looked upon politics as a science rather than a business; He adopts his maxims as he finds them in books, and with too little regard to the actual state of things."[12] Putting it in even stronger terms, he averred, "This is not the form nor the occasion to discharge our obligations of any sort to any foreign nation, it concerns not our feelings but our interests, yet the debate has often soared high above the smoke of business into the

---

10 Henry Cabot Lodge, *Life and Letters of George Cabot* (Little Brown, 1878), p. 76

11 *Ibid.* p. 1628

12 Ames to George Minor, May 3, 1789

epic region."[13]

No aspect of Madison disturbed Ames more than the Virginian's campaign to establish high duties on goods arriving in British ships. Ames believed that the proposal could only lead to economic war or war itself. The New Englanders were men of business, and as such they desired stability. Ames's question:

> But are we Yankees invulnerable, if a war of regulations should be waged with Britain? Are they not able to retaliate? . . . Is it not more prudent to maintain a good understanding with Great Britain, and to preserve a dignified neutrality and moderation of conduct towards all nations?[14]

Madison was also interested in doing business, but doing in such a way that it would benefit the United States, not England. He based his argument on three points: first, that Great Britain must be forced into a more equitable relationship, one that would admit American wheat, flour, and salted provisions, second, British dominance posed the danger that she would use her position to disrupt American commerce, and finally, Madison spoke of the influence "that may finally ensue on our taste, our manners, and on our form of government itself."[15] This last point was the essence of the arguments made by both Madison and Jefferson, they did not wish to become British with its rule by the well born in the new Republic.

The difficulty was, according to Madison, that the United States had already become servile to Great Britain. He particularly objected to the argument that implementation of his resolutions would reduce the revenue and endanger the public credit. While he had no desire to destroy the present funding system he held that "it was never either meant by Congress, or understood by the public, that, in mortgaging the impost for their security, it was to be hostage

---

13 Annals of Congress, 3rd Cong, 1st sess., p. 340

14 *Ibid.*, July 3, 1789

15 Annals of Congress, 3d Cong.1st sess, p. 215

to foreign countries for our unqualified acquiescence in their unequal laws, and to be worn, as long as the Debt should continue, as a badge of national humiliation."[16]

The difficulties with Great Britain had been building since the end of the American Revolution. In November, 1791, Thomas Pinckney had been appointed by Washington as the first minister of the United States to the Court of St. James. At the same time, The British sent George Hammond to America as its first minister to the United States. Pinckney was a Federalist, and not an experienced diplomat, rather he was a South Carolina planter who had served one term as its governor. Hammond on the other hand was an experienced diplomat and was quick to sound out the political temper of the leading Americans, especially Hamilton. Because of his American connections, Hammond came to the opinion that Pinckney could be counted among the "party of the British interest," i.e., those who had opposed any specific discriminations on British commerce and who advocated generally closer relationships between the two countries on the basis of the *status quo*.

In a letter to The British Foreign Minister, Lord Grenville, Hammond expressed his opinion of Pinckney:

> Those persons of this country who are desirous of promoting and preserving a good understanding with Great Britain are extremely well satisfied with Mr. Pinckney's appointment as they consider the circumstance of his education at Westminster School, and of having passed a great part of his life in England, as having a natural tendency to inspire him with a predilection for the country, and a desire of rendering his conduct satisfactory.[17]

Basically, Pinckney was given very few instructions other than expressing "that spirit of sincere friendship which we bear to the

16 Paul A. Varg, *New England and Foreign Relations, 1789-1850* (Hanover, New Hampshire: University Press of New England, 1983) , p. 21

17 Hammond to Grenville, Jan. 2, 1792

English nation," since matters of importance between the United States and Britain were handled by Jefferson and Hammond. The exception was to protect American seamen from the press gangs in British ports.[18]

The British court and diplomatic core at this time seemed to hold the United States, by virtue of the example of the American Revolution, somewhat responsible for the European convulsions brought on by the French Revolution. Consequently, Americans were not considered desirable associates. Pinckney noted on this situation, "At the same time they have been polite enough to make themselves a proper distinction between the modes of conducting the revolutions in the two countries."[19]

Pinckney's work concerning impressment give us a glimpse into the beginning of this notable and insoluble issue. Since the American war for Independence there had been little occasion for the press gang in British ports, but when the possibility of a British war with Spain arose, a press of seamen occurred, including several American sailors. Although the seamen were eventually released, the expense and inconvenience to the American government in liberating the impressed sailors and possibly the indefensible character of the outrage impelled Jefferson to adopt some arrangement to prevent impressment whenever another European crisis should occur.[20] Gouverneur Morris, an American statesman and Founding Father suggested in 1790 that American sailors in British territorial waters be furnished with certificates of citizenship as a protection. Jefferson rejected this proposition and suggested that British pressgangs might be permitted to board an American ship in a British port only when the crew of that ship was ascertained, by a previous visit of a strictly limited number of officers, to have more than an agreed proportion of hands to her tonnage. He actually authorized Pinckney to agree to

---

18 Jefferson to Pinckney, June 11, 1792

19 Same to same, Dec. 13, 1792

20 Jefferson to Washington, Feb. 7, 1792

an article of convention on such a basis.[21]

Pinckney, realized that if Great Britain became involved the European wars then raging, there would be an immediate need for an increase in the number of British sailors. When the war with France did begin, British captains began to take alleged British subjects from the decks of American ships without careful distinction between territorial waters and the high seas. In February, 1793, Pinckney went to Lord Grenville about the problem of impressment. Grenville, in an effort to put Pinckney off sent him to Phineas Bond, a British counsel-general to Philadelphia then on vacation in England, who had no power to solve the problem. Bond suggested the old idea of the United States furnishing its' seamen with certificates of citizenship. In a letter to Jefferson, Pinckney outlined his reply to Bond, attempting to equate the two country's problems:

I told him the inconveniences arising from this procedure (certificates) would be equally felt by both nations, for that we should expect their seamen to be furnished with similar testimonials when they come to our ports to those they expected our mariners would bring to theirs; he asked in what instance it could become necessary (alluding I presume to our not being in the habit of impressing). I answered that unless we could come to some accommodation which might insure our seamen against this oppression measures would be taken to cause the inconvenience to be equally felt on both sides.[22]

Having no success with Bond, Pinckney began to give up attempting to solve the problem. Writing about this to Jefferson in April:

I have no hope of obtaining at present any convention respecting seamen, as Lord Grenville now says it is necessary for them to make enquiries as to some points in America, which object is given in charge to Mr. Bond. The impressment on the present occasion has not been so detrimental to our trade as it

---

21 Jefferson to Pinckney, June 11, 1792

22 Pinckney to Jefferson, March 13, 1793

was on former occasions, though several instances of hardship have occurred which I have endeavor'd [sic]to remedy but not always with success.[23]

In his reply to Pinckney, Jefferson regarded this failure to be of a "serious nature indeed," but decided "to hazard no further reflection on the subject through the present channel of consequences."[24]

When Congress assembled in Philadelphia in March 1793 the western world was experiencing the turbulence of the French Revolution. The Jacobins and Robespierre ruled Paris, the Reign of Terror was nearing its peak, and France, the nation in arms, was at war with her neighbors. In May, Washington issued his Neutrality Proclamation and also In May the British took the French West Indian islands of Tobago, St. Pierre, and Miquelon. The English planters on the islands formerly remitted their profits in sugar to France, now the money would go directly to England. With these islands under British control, the American lucrative trade with the West Indies would now came under the British Navigation Acts.[25] Additionally the British promulgated a series of orders-in-council restricting neutral trade, including foodstuffs resulting in the seizure of some 250 American ships by March 1794.

The American merchant marine received its first blow on June 8, 1793, when the British cabinet decreed an Order in Council according to which all neutral ships heading to France and carrying wheat or flour were to be brought into British ports so that the cargo could be seized and purchased by the British government. The Order in Council which constituted a threat to the American merchant

---

23 Ibid., April 4, 1793

24 Jefferson to Pinckney, June 2, 1793

25 The Acts apply the 'rule of 1756' barring neutrals from trade with belligerents' colonies in wartime if that trade was proscribed in peace. It made American trade in the West Indies at least susceptible to British colonial taxation, if not the seizure and confiscation of their ships. Also, the French planters who fled the islands, traveled mainly to the United States where they settled in large numbers in Philadelphia, the American capital, promoting French opinions and policy

marine also endangered the interests of American farmers. Another Order in Council was issued on November 6, 1793 was intended to sever relations between France and its colonies by prohibiting neutral powers from transporting colonial products: "all ships laden with goods [that are] the produce of any colony belonging to France, or carrying provisions or other supplies for the use of any such colony" were to be stopped and detained, and brought in "for prize-court adjudication."[26] This action violated the principle of "free ship makes free goods," in other words if the ship was not a belligerent (e.g. neutral) then the ship's cargo was not subject to capture by a belligerent.[27]

The continuing problem for the United States was that as important as the seizure of American ships and cargoes was, the impressment of its seamen was the more important issue. This forcible capture of American seamen by the British Royal Navy in the late 18th century was regarded by the United States as a deliberate and cowardly act perpetrated by a foreign power against innocent men. This action by the British stoked popular outrage, provoking Congress and raising diplomatic tensions with Britain.

Impressment constituted a long-standing tradition in Great Britain as the nation evolved into a strong seafaring nation. The Royal Navy had the chronic situation of not having enough crews to man their ships, especially during wartime and so began to view impressment as a legitimate method of recruitment. By the 18th century, Britain came to regard impressment as a maritime right and extended the practice to boarding neutral merchant ships in local waters and at sea.

In the 1790s, impressment became even more important as the outbreak of war between Britain and France in the wake of the

---

26 Samuel Bemis, *Jay's Treaty, A Study in Commerce and Diplomacy* (New Haven: Yale University Press, 1923), p. 158

27 Nevertheless, as a principle of international law (apart from treaty law), this principle was ignored by both France and Great Britain, although adhered to by the United States.

French Revolution created the need for a much larger English navy. Between 1793 and 1812, Parliament increased the size of the Royal Navy from 135 to 584 ships and expanded their crews from 36,000 to 114,000 seamen. By contrast, manpower in the British merchant marine in 1792 already stood at 118,000, reflecting a noticeable preferment for civilian over military service by seamen.

The practice immediately drew Britain into ideological conflict with the recently established government of the United States. Tempered by generations of local self-rule and individual freedoms, America strenuously disavowed impressment as an international right. This perceived flouting of freedom on the part of the British also clashed directly with America's emerging attitude regarding the rights of neutrals on the high seas. The United States, attempting to assert itself as an emerging naval power, not only championed the right of neutrals to engage in free trade with belligerents at war but also believed that neutrality protected all persons sailing under a sovereign flag regardless of national origin. As Secretary of State James Madison observed to James Monroe in 1804, who was then serving as United States' minister to Great Britain, "We consider a neutral flag on the high seas as a safeguard to those sailing under it. . . [N]owhere will she [Great Britain] find an exception to this freedom of the seas, and of neutral ships, which justifies the taking away of any person not an enemy in military service, found a board a neutral vessel."[28] The right of visitation and search, Americans maintained, should allow for a cursory examination of a vessel's papers or manifest, but preclude the seizure of neutral civilians.

To meet the problem of the seizure of American ships and the impressment of its seamen, the Republicans put forth two Congressional measures in April 1794. The first called for a sequestration of debts owed to British citizens, the second, an embargo on trade with Great Britain. While the first measure never came to a vote. On the embargo, the Federalists argued that it would merely serve to cause Great Britain to strike back with

---

28 James Madison to James Monroe, February 5, 1806

countermeasures, since it would be viewed as a threat. While the New England members of Congress received support from members in other states, in those areas there were differences of opinion, not so in New England, which was on the verge of becoming a one party section committed to a sound credit and currency system, to economic stability, and to a federal government that would serve the merchant and shipping interests.

The New Englanders were clearly in the right, the proposed Republican stand against England and in favor of France would not have moved the British toward a more generous policy in dealing with the United States nor would it have resulted in a major expansion of trade with France. The financial condition of the United States also argued against entering into economic warfare with Britain. In 1794, the infant Republic stood on the verge of financial bankruptcy. Not only did the United States have a large number of government bonds outstanding, but the treasury was only able to meet the interest charges by negotiating short-term loans in England. Also since the European wars had created financial problems in London, if the Americans pressed to hard, the British could have cut off future short-term loans.

The winter of 1794 brought the United States close to war with England. There was continued pressure on the government from the Republicans to use provocative measures against the British, coupled with the actions of the British themselves; the seizure of American ships, their occupation of military posts in the American West, and their dominance of the nation's trade. In an attempt to solve the problem, four Federalists Senators; Oliver Ellsworth of Connecticut, George Cabot and Caleb Strong of Massachusetts, and Rufus King of New York met to discuss how they might advise the president. Their recommendation was that American defenses be strengthened and that an envoy be sent to England to negotiate.[29] It wasn't only the Federalists who were feeling the pressure. In late August

---

29 Harold Syrett, ed., *The Papers of Alexander Hamilton*, 44 vols. (New York: Columbia University Press, 1972), 16: p. 132-133

1793, a Committee of merchants in Philadelphia published in the *Philadelphia Federal Gazette* a letter from Secretary of State Thomas Jefferson and their answer to it:

> "The Govt. has received your complaint of spoliation committed on your merchant ships by privateers of the warring European powers. The president has asked me to assure all merchants involved in foreign trade and navigation that we will seek to redress for all injuries they sustain on the high seas or in foreign countries contrary to the Law of Nations or our existing treaties.

> Forward your authenticated evidence to us and we will institute the proper proceedings for your relief. The just and friendly disposition of the belligerents persuade us that they will take effectual measures to restrain their armed vessels from committing aggression on our citizens or their property. Please publish this to whoever is a victim of such spoliation. You may send your complaints as individuals or associations."

Apparently, the merchants did not trust that the problem would be solved, their answer:

> "We have been strictly neutral and friendly to everyone and we ought to be exempt from these depredations."

> Sgd John Nixon[30]

Washington agreed that a treaty with the British was the only option and Chief Justice John Jay, a Federalist, was sent to England to do the negotiations amidst suspicion and charges that he was an Anglophile. It was however Hamilton who not only wrote Jay's formal instructions but also gave him detailed advice in private letters. Hamilton realized the weakness of the American position, Jay's only significant bargaining chip in the negotiations was the threat that the United States would join the Danish and Swedish governments

---

30 *Philadelphia Federal Gazette*, August 31, 1793

in defending their neutral status and resisting British seizure of their goods by force of arms. Hamilton independently informed the British leadership that the United States had no intention of joining in this neutral armament. Hamilton's actions left Jay with little leverage to force the British to comply with American demands. Actually, the only two cards that the Americans could possibly play was an alliance with the French, and the loss of an economic trading partner, the British. Since Great Britain was basically alone in its European struggles, it would have had to split its forces to also do battle once more with the United States. Perhaps, this is why Jay was well received by the British in November of 1793.

As far as Alexander Hamilton was concerned, with the resignation of Thomas Jefferson, Hamilton became in effect, the Secretary of State, and as a committed Anglophile, he wanted a treaty, any treaty which would have avoided war between the countries and bound the two nations closer together. Hamilton had to believe that the British would not stop impressing American seaman and seizing American ships, but with an agreement, the Federalist Party would become predominant and the United States would be joined to Great Britain, even though the 1778 treaty with France would be in many ways nullified.

The essence of Republican opposition to the treaty that Jay negotiated centered around the repercussions that the treaty would have on the foreign relations of the United States. Many Republicans suspected that the proposed agreement was the first step towards an alliance with Great Britain. "The treaty from one end to the other must be regarded as a demonstration that the Party to which the Envoy belongs . . .," said James Madison, "is a British party systematically aiming at an exclusive connection with the British Government."[31] "Americanus" in the *Virginia Gazette and General Advertiser* denounced the treaty as "a base unnatural political connection between a Republican government and Monarchy."[32]

---

31 James Madison to Robert Livingston, August 10, 1795

32 *Virginia Gazette and General Advertiser*, July 17, 1795

Said a meeting of the inhabitants of Fayette County, Kentucky: "The alliance of such a corrupt, degenerate & stinking people, ought religiously to be avoided by the American people."[33] Thomas Jefferson, the former Secretary of State, viewing recent events from the quiet of Monticello, argued that Jay's Treaty was in fact an alliance. The treaty, said Jefferson, "is nothing more than a treaty of alliance between England & the Anglomen of this country against the legislature & people of the United States."[34]

Jefferson and his fellow Republicans were determined to prevent a realignment of the United States within the British system. Such an alliance would antagonize the French with whom Great Britain was at war. A rupture of Franco-American relations Republicans believed would be "a circumstance not to be contemplated without horror."[35] For was not France, asked "A Young Patriot" in the *Richmond and Manchester Advertiser*, the nation which recently "rescued you from slavery, your wives from insult and violation, and your children from butchery?"[36] And for that matter, were not the French still in 1795 fighting for liberty and equality against the redcoats of George III? In Republican minds, American liberties were inextricably bound up with the destiny of France and both American liberties and French integrity were fearfully menaced by the combined despots of Europe. The issue in 1795 was the issue of 1776, still freedom versus slavery, still France against "the common enemy of the liberties of mankind."[37]

The Republicans also believed that there was more to the treaty than to ally Great Britain with the United States, there was also the possibility that the treaty would foist upon the nation a despotism like the British monarchy. Republicans assumed that the Federalists were a monarchial and aristocratic party "whose avowed object is

33 Resolves of Fayette County, Kentucky, August 28, 1795

34 Thomas Jefferson to Edward Rutledge, November 30, 1795

35 Resolves of Portsmouth, Virginia, August 5, 1795

36 *Richmond and Manchester Advertiser*, October 10, 1795

37 *Virginia Gazette and General Advertiser*, May 28, 1794

to draw over us the substance, as they have already done the forms, of the British government."[38] The treaty was the work of such "a vile aristocratic few who have too long governed America, and who are enemies to the equality of man."[39] Virginian William Wilson summed up Republican arguments against the settlement:

> To be dragooned into a treaty with barbarians, who the other day were laying this Country in smoke and ashes – and are at this day committing every Species of piratical depredations that robbers can Suggest. For the Citizens of America to be degraded by an Instrument, obtained by British influence, and calculated to make this Republic a party with the coalesced monsters, against a Nation which has so lately save us from gibbets & confiscation, has secured to us liberty, - Independence & Sovereignty, And now the only friend we have in the Scale of Nations. To submit to this, and to become the felons of our own Constitution, would be Synonomous [sic] terms.[40]

The Jay Treaty ended the drift toward war and therein lay its great merit. Its provisions, taken singly, were subject to just criticisms, but the treaty as a whole prevented war with Great Britain until the United States was in a stronger military position. Those who supported the treaty readily admitted that Great Britain had dealt harshly and sharply with the United States, but they were not ready to brace themselves for economic warfare. This would have interrupted the growth of trade and reduced the prosperity that they had recently experienced. The New England merchant and shipbuilding community dominated the section politically. But more was involved, their fear of the Jacobins and the republican societies at home was greater than their fear of Great Britain.[41]

---

38 Jefferson to Philip Mazzei, April 24, 1796

39 Lexington *Kentucky Gazette*, September 14, 1795

40 William Wilson to Joseph Jones, September 14, 1795, Joseph Jones Papers, Duke University.

41 Paul A. Varg, New England and Foreign Relation, 1789-1850, p. 17

When the treaty that Jay had negotiated reached the president, the only motive that could have prevented Washington from signing it was his mistrust of the former enemy in the War for Independence. Seeing that the treaty was likely to be sent back to Great Britain for further negotiation, Edmund Randolph, Jefferson's successor as secretary of state and the last Republican member of the cabinet wrote to James Monroe, then serving as American minister to Paris on July 14, 1795 that "The treaty is not yet ratified by the president nor will it be ratified, I believe, until it returns from England, if then.[42]Little did Randolph imagine that barely one month later, he would bring about that which he feared most, the signing of the treaty by President Washington. The British in an attack on a French vessel, intercepted a letter from the French minister to the United States, Joseph Fauchet to Randolph which allegedly revealed that Randolph had criticized other members of the cabinet and more importantly, that Randolph was looking for financial aid to rekindle Republican party control of western political leaders in the area in which the president had just put down the Whiskey Rebellion. The letter from Fauchet finished, "Thus a few thousand dollars would have been enough for the French republic to decide the issue between war and peace. It is true that the certainty of these painful conclusions will remain indefinitely within our archives."[43]

For Washington, this was all the proof needed to accuse Randolph of siding with the rebels in the western United States. On August 19, 1795, Washington showed the letter to Randolph, and without looking into the matter, refused to accept his explanations. As a result of this incident, Randolph resigned, thus removing the last Republican from Washington's cabinet.[44]

The reason for the alarm and anxiety of the Washington

42 Randolph to Monroe, July 14, 1795.

43 Dispatch no. 10, Oct. 31, 1794 in Correspondance Politique Etats-Unis, vol. 42 folois 125-126

44 Samuel Bemis, *The American Secretaries of State and their Diplomacy* (New York: Cooper Square Press, 1927), p. 81

Administration was the spontaneous organization of democratic-republican societies. Heirs of the Sons of Liberty and Committees of Correspondence that had been established to support the Revolution, these groups were being established throughout the nation, numbering thirty-five by the middle of 1795. While the new groups were based on former American organizations, they were also similar to the French Jacobin clubs, although without the violence. Also the societies openly supported the French Revolution, which engendered fear among the Federalists.

An examination of these groups showed that the Federalists had some cause for concern, because the societies believed that the administration was insensitive to their wishes, especially in respect to revolutionary France. One New York democratic-republican society flatly declared that "he who is an enemy to the French revolution . . . ought not to be entrusted with the guidance of any part of the machine of government."[45]

The popularity of these societies however was short lived because it was believed by the general public that they were associated with the so called Whiskey Rebellion, even though the societies denounced the violence associated with it.

Washington however believed in the connection between the societies and the Whiskey Rebellion openly denouncing them in August by attacking them as "the most diabolical attempts to destroy the best fabric of human government and happiness that has ever been presented for the acceptance of mankind." He also blamed Genet for "having . . . brought the eggs of these venomous reptiles to our shores..." [46]

In the fall of 1794, Washington again publicly accused the societies of supporting the whiskey rebels, saying that he feared them

---

45 Philip S. Foner, *The Democratic-Republican Societies, 1790-1800: A Documentary Sourcebook of Constitutions, Declarations, Addresses, Resolutions, and Toasts* (Westport, Conn.: Greenwood Press, 1976), p. 22

46 Washington to Henry Lee, August 26, 1794

to be linked to French intrigue "to sow sedition [and] poison the minds of the people of this country."[47]

While the Congress was split into two factions, for the Federalists to reach their goal of total control of the Executive Branch of the government, they needed only to remove Monroe from his position as ambassador to France.

Monroe had taken his position in France early in 1794, at the height of the Anglo-American crisis. His instructions from Randolph were to keep close relations with France, the only major America ally, especially in light of the coming publication of Jay's treaty that Randolph knew was being negotiated. When the news of the treaty reached both Monroe and the French Committee of Public Safety, Monroe wrote to Randolph, "Mr. Jay had not only adjusted the points in controversy, but concluded a treaty of commerce with that government. Some of these accounts state that he had also concluded a treaty of alliance, offensive and defensive." Monroe was also anxious to quell the doubts that arose in his own mind as he wondered whether he was not the "organ of . . . a double and perfidious policy," sent to Paris to allay French suspicions until an Anglo-American treaty was signed."[48] As an example of the enmity between the two American factions, when Monroe asked Jay for a copy of the treaty, Jay refused since he placed no trust in the Republicans, who, in his view only wanted to sell out the United States to France.[49] Once the treaty became known, not only did Monroe cease to receive instructions from Washington, but he became an impotent witness to French wrath. In the pages of the French newspaper, *Moniteur*, an editorial put the French ire in perspective:

---

47 Lloyd S. Kramer, The French Revolution and the Creation of the American Political Culture, in Joseph Klaits and Michael H. Haltzel (eds), *The Global Ramifications of the French Revolution* (Cambridge: Cambridge University Press, 2002), p. 37. Kramer argues that the French Revolution was the most influential international event affecting the United States with the exception of the two world wars, the cold war, and the Vietnam.

48 Monroe to Randolph, January 13, 1795 & December 18, 1794;

49 James Monroe to the Secretary of State, March 17, 1795

Indeed, there were dangers for you to face; but was there not only also a sacred debt to be paid off, and national honor to be defended? Who held up your forts and captured your vessels? England did. Who sought to enslave you? Who brought you to war with Algerians and the Indians? England did. And who defended you when you broke your chains? France did. Who, for her own sake, wants you to preserve your liberty? France does.[50]

If the situation for Monroe was not bad enough, Randolph's successor as secretary of state, Thomas Pickering, a Federalist, blamed Monroe for the problems with France, which was ludicrous since Monroe had never even read the treaty, much less had any involvement in it. On top of this, in a letter dated August 22, 1796, Pickering recalled Monroe, thus ending any executive power that the Republicans had, giving total control to the Federalists who could now implement their policies.

Washington submitted the treaty to the Senate for ratification in June 1795. Its' initial unpopularity gave the Republicans a platform to rally new supporters One opinion of the treaty was that its' major problem was not that the treaty was an international problem, but an internal one. "The Jay Treaty was a reasonable give-and-take compromise spelled out between the two countries. What rendered it so assailable was not the compromise spelled out between the two nations but the fact that it was not a compromise between the two political parties at home. Embodying the views of the Federalists, the treaty repudiated the foreign policy of the opposing party.[51]

Contemporary historians had a variety of evaluations of the treaty:

The fierce debates over the Treaty in 1794-95 according to William Nisbet Chambers, "transformed the Republican

---

50 *La MoniteurUniversel* 6 ventosean 4 (February 25, 1796)), vol. 127. no. 166

51 Paul Varg, *Foreign Policies of the Founding Fathers* (East Lansing: Michigan State University Press, 1963), p. 95

movement into a Republican Party." To fight the treaty the Jeffersonians "established coordination in activity between leaders at the capital, and leaders, actives and popular followings in the states, counties, and towns"[52]

Historian Marshall Smelser argues that the treaty effectively postponed war with Britain for ten years and more.[53]

Bradford Perkins opined that the treaty was the first installment of a special relationship between Britain and America. In his view, the treaty worked for ten years to secure peace between the two nations: The decade may be characterized as the period of "The First Rapprochement." "For about ten years, there was peace on the frontier, joint recognition of the value of commercial intercourse, and even, by comparison with both preceding and succeeding epochs, a muting of strife over ship seizures and impressment. Two controversies with France. . . . pushed the English speaking powers even more closely together." He concludes, "Through a decade of world war and peace, successive governments on both sides of the Atlantic were able to bring about and preserve a cordiality which often approached genuine friendship."[54]

Joseph Ellis finds the treaty "one-sided in Britain's favor," but agrees with other historians that it was "a shrewd bargain for the United States. It bet, in effect on England rather than France as the hegemonic European power of the future, which proved prophetic. It recognized the massive dependence of the American economy on trade with England. In a sense it was a precocious preview of the Monroe Doctrine (1823) for it linked American security and economic development to the British fleet, which provided a protective shield of incalculable value throughout the nineteenth

---

52 William Nisbet Chambers, *Political Parties in a New Nation: The American Experience, 1776-1809* (Oxford: Oxford University Press, 1963), p. 80

53 Marshall Smelser, *The Democratic Republic: 1801-1815* (New York: Harper Collins, 1968), p. 139

54 Bradford Perkins, *The First Rapprochement: England and the United States, 1795-1805* (Oakland: University of California Press, 1955), p. vii & 1

century. Mostly, it postponed war with England until America was economically and politically more capable of fighting one."[55]

And a very negative opinion from L.S. Kaplan. "When Jay was dispatched to London, his major mission was to end British depredations on the high seas. The treaty he signed not only had nothing to say on the subject but also appeared to accept the British depredations of neutral rights and freedom of the seas. British interpretations of international law were written into the treaty. Nor did Jay secure the commercial treaty Hamilton had wanted or the privileges such a treaty would have accorded American commerce, with the exception of a limited entry into the West Indies which was so inadequate that Article VII, in which it was embodied, was deleted by the Senate. Conspicuous by its silence in the treaty was the flaming issue of impressment. . . .Westerners were upset over Jay's failure to gain a British commitment against interference in Indian affairs in the Northwest, while Southerners were angry over his failure to provide compensation for the loss of slave property carried away by the British army during the war.[56]

Ratification of the Jay Treaty and the alleged[57] revelations of Randolph's anti-Americanism left the Franco-American treaty in shreds. In the course of 1795, French warships captured and sold more than three hundred American ships and their cargoes without

---

55 Joseph Ellis, *Founding Brothers: The Revolutionary Generation* (New York: Vintage Books, 2000),p. 136-137

56 L. S. Kaplan, *Colonies into Nation: American Diplomacy, 1763-1801* (New York: Macmillan, 1972), p. 241-242

57 Randolph's letter of resignation included the assertion "I here most solemnly deny that any overture ever came to me which was to produce money to me, or any others for me; and that in any manner, directly or indirectly, was a shilling ever received by me. Nor was it ever contemplated by me that one shilling should be applied by Mr. Fauchet to any purpose relative to the insurrection." Randolph later published a 103 page pamphlet entitled "A Vindication," proving his innocence, but it so insulted Washington that it failed to restore Randolph in the public trust. Richard Harwell, *Washington, An abridgement in one volume of the seven volume George Washington* by Douglas Southall Freeman (New York: Charles Scribner's Sons, 1968), p. 678-689

compensating the owners and they committed untold atrocities against captured American seaman – either executing them at sea or placing them in the Bordeaux prison.

The French however did make an effort to temper the American's government towards France in the person of their new Ambassador to the United States, Pierre August Adet. Unfortunately, Adet began his duties by bringing up the old issues that Genet and Fauchet had raised – advance repayment of American Revolutionary War debts to France and allowing French privateers to use American ports. Adet had received a copy of the Jay treaty from Fauchet which stated that when the treaty was ratified by the American Senate, not only would the French privateers still be excluded, but now English privateers would be allowed in American ports. When Washington signed the treaty, Adet assailed both the president and the Senate, "The President has just signed the dishonor of his old age, and the shame of the United States; he had ratified the Treaty of Commerce and Amenity with Great Britain . . . and pledged [his] blind submission to the supreme will of [King] George."[58] Adet went even further sending a copy of the treaty to the pro-French newspaper *Aurora* to publish. As Adet had hoped, America's Republicans and Francophiles arose as one, raging that the Jay Treaty "insidiously aims to dissolve all connections between the United States and France, and to substitute a monarchic for a republican ally."[59] Even Jefferson, although out of office at the time weighted in writing to his friend Philip Mazzei:

In place of that noble love of liberty & republican government which carried us triumphantly thro' the war, an anglican, monarchical & aristocratical party has sprung up whose avowed object is to draw over us. . . the forms of British government. . . . Against us are the Executive, the Judiciary . . . . all the officers of the government, all who want to be officers, all timid men who prefer calm despotism to

58 Nouvelle BiographeGeneraledepuis les Temps les PlusReculesjusqu'a Nos Jours, 1:278-279; Dictionnaire de la BiographieFrancaise, 1:574-576

59 Alexander DeConde, *Entangling Alliance* (Durham: N.C.: Duke University Press, 1958), p. 554

the boisterous sea of liberty, British merchants & Americans trading on British capital, speculators & holders in the banks & public funds, a contrivance for the purposes of corruption & and for assimilating us in all things, to the rotten as well as the sound parts of the British model.[60]

Jefferson continued his vilification of Washington and the Federalists later on in the same letter, "It would give you a fever were I to name to you the apostates who have gone over to these heresies, men who were Samsons in the field and Solomans in the councils, but who have had their heads shorn by the harlot England."[61]

The Jay Treaty between the United States and England in 1795 was a major factor in accelerating a degenerating relationship between the former allies, France and the United States. The agreement, which represented a failed American effort to get England to accept the United States' position that free ships means free goods, appeared to many to not only insult France, but to tie America more closely to France's enemy, England.[62]

When the Jay Treaty took effect early in 1796, the French government repudiated the Franco-American treaties of 1778, and also changed its tactics in dealing with the United States. The new French Foreign Minister, Charles Delacroix now instructed Adet to eschew subterfuge and "use all the means in his power in the United States to bring about a successful revolution and Washington's replacement."[63] Delacroix told Adet to mobilize Americans against the Jay Treaty and Washington's policy of neutrality. "There is not an instant to lose in attaching the [American] nation to France

---

60 Dumas Malone, *Jefferson and the Ordeal of Liberty* (Boston: Little Brown & Co., 1963), p. 267

61 *Ibid.* p. 267-268

62 Manuela Albertone & Antonino De Francesco (eds.), *Rethinking the Atlantic World: Europe and America in the Age of Democratic Revolutions* (London: Palgrave Macmillan, 2009), p. 211

63 Archives des Affairs ErrangeresMinistere des Affaires Etrangeres, Paris Etats-Unis, vol. XLV

in the war against England and Spain, the conquest of Canada and Louisiana must be made this very winter; fleets of privateers, sustained by our warships must go and destroy the commerce of our mutual enemies."[64]

On September 19, 1796, President Washington announced that he would retire at the end of his second term. Although he had decided to retire almost six months earlier he had kept the decision to himself to limit the time for electioneering that he believed might divide the nation and provoke insurrection or civil war because of the two growing factions – the Federalists and the Democratic-Republicans. The "President's Farewell Address" to the nation appeared in the *American Daily Advertiser* in Philadelphia. Part of the Address contained these words defending his policy of neutrality along with a warning:

Against the insidious wiles of foreign influence, I conjure you to believe me, fellow citizens, the jealousy of a free people ought to be constantly awake. . . . Even our commercial policy should hold an equal and impartial hand. . . .Tis folly in one nation to look for disinterested favors from another . . . There can be no greater error than to expect or calculate upon real favors from nation to nation.[65]

Since Washington decided not to run for reelection, Adet again changed tactics, instead of inciting revolution in the streets, he now pursued the course of attaining his ends through the democratic process, he would now back a noted Francophile, Thomas Jefferson for the American presidency. His method was to use the American press to campaign for Jefferson, continuously warning that only a Jefferson victory would prevent war with France. The controversy became so heated that the Federalists and the Republicans began to refer to themselves as the French or British Party.

---

64 Meade Minnigerode, *Jefferson, Friend of France* (New York: G.P. Putnam & Sons, 1928),p. 347

65 Richard Harwell, *Washington, An abridgement in one volume of the seven-volume George Washington* by Douglas Southall Freeman, p. 701-702

In November, 1796, Adet began what became known as cockade proclamation, which called on French citizens and friends of France to wear the red, white, and blue cockade.[66]Across the nation, Democratic Societies sent members into the streets to pin cockades on passersby – sometimes by force. French flags appeared in windows everywhere, along with signs calling for union with France. Pennsylvania Quakers grew so fearful of war with France they unanimously voted for Jefferson and the Republicans.

"French influence never appeared so open and unmasked", South Carolina congressman William Loughton Smith wrote to Hamilton, who had left government to practice law in New York. "French flags, French cockades were displayed by the Jefferson party and there is no doubt that French money was spred. . . . In short there was never so barefaced and disgraceful an interference of a foreign power in any free country."[67]

Although Washington assailed Adet's "meddling in American politics," he had no way of stopping the Frenchman. On November 15, 1796, Adet issued his final, most menacing warning to the secretary of state, he called "the treaty of commerce concluded with Great Britain equivalent to a treaty of alliance" and said that it had so offended the French government that it had sent him orders "to suspend from this moment, his ministerial functions with the Federal Government" – in effect breaking diplomatic relations with the United States. But in an astonishing addendum, he appealed to the people – as Genet had threatened to do –with a declaration that:

The American people are not to regard the suspension of his ministerial functions as a rupture between France and the United States, but as a mark of discontent, which is to last until the Government of the United States returns to sentiments, and to

---

66 A cockade is a knot of colored ribbons or an oval shaped symbol usually worn on a hat. In the 18th and 19th centuries they were used in Europe to show the allegiance of their wearers to some political faction.

67 Archives des Affaires Errangeres, Ministere des Affaires Enangeres, Paris, Etats-Unis, vol. XLV

measures, more comfortable to the interests of the alliance, and the sworn friendship between the two nations . . . this alliance has always been dear to Frenchmen, they have done everything to tighten its bands. The Government of the United States, on the contrary, has sought to break them. . . . Let your Government return to itself, and you will still find in Frenchmen faithful friends and genuine allies.[68]

Relations between the two nations continued to deteriorate, in addition to the French government recalling Adet, they also not only refused to receive America's new ambassador, Charles Pinckney, but expelled him from France as an undesirable foreigner. Instead of returning to the United States, Pinckney took refuge in Holland where John Quincy Adams, the vice president's son was ambassador. Adams said of the situation, "There is a great ignorance of the character and sentiments of the American people in France among those who imagine that any manoeuvre of theirs could turn an election against the President of the United States."[69]

As Adams predicted, Adet's words had the opposite effect, Federalist newspapers across the North demonized Adet and warned that a Jefferson presidency would be "fatal to our independence, now that the interference of a foreign nation in our affairs is no longer disguised."[70] The *Connecticut Courant* called Adet's press campaign an attempt to "wean us from the government and administrators of our own choice and make us willing to be governed by such as France shall think best for us – beginning with Jefferson." New York newspaper editor, Noah Webster writing in the Federalist paper *American Minerva,* asked "how long the delicacy of our government will suffer every species of indignity from the agents of the French nation in this country?"[71] Further, referring to France, Webster wrote

---

68 Adet to Secretary of State Thomas Pickering, November 15,1796, American State Papers, Foreign Relations, I:579-583

69 John Quincy Adams to Joseph Pitcarin, November 13, 1796

70 Dumas Malone, *Ordeal of Liberty,* p. 288

71 John C. Miller, *The Federalist Era, 1789-1901* (New York: Harper & Brothers, 1967), p. 196-197

that:

> An open enemy is less dangerous than an *insidious friend*.
> . . . Interest is the pole star of their conduct; such it has proved
> in every stage of their connections with us. Have they not told
> us themselves, that they will not regard their treaties if they
> afterwards discover them to be disadvantageous? Americans
> have more to fear from the French than from the English.
> The French. . . .are determined to *have* a ruling influence, and
> control over the councils of our nation, and over the good
> people of the United States. . . .the first words our children
> should see in the primer, after WORSHIP thy CREATOR,
> ought to be NO FOREIGN INFLUENCE.[72]

To give an example of the seriousness that both sides took
with this issue, the Jeffersonian Republicans fought back referring
to Webster as "a pusillanimous, half-begotten, self-dubbed patriot,"
an incurable lunatic," and "a deceitful newsmonger . . . Pedagogue
and Quack."[73]

The Republicans however were also beginning to worry about
the actions of the French government. One spoke out that Adet's
meddling had destroyed Jefferson's chances for election and that the
electors would "sooner be shot than vote for him." Another that Adet
had "irretrievably diminished the good will felt for his Government
and the people of France by most people here."[74] By the end of 1796,
Adet, who was not making much progress, now began to question
Jefferson's loyalty to France. "I do not know if . . . we shall always
find in him a man wholly devoted to our interests. Mr. Jefferson likes
us because he detests England; he seeks to draw near to us because he
fears us less than Great Britain; but he might change his opinion of
us tomorrow, if tomorrow Great Britain should cease to inspire his

---

72 *American Minerva*, April 11, 1794

73 Joseph Ellis, *After the Revolution: Profiles of Early American Culture* (New York:
W.W. Norton & Company Inc., 2002), p. 199

74 Alexander DeConde, *Entangling Alliance*, p. 476

fears. . . . Jefferson is American and as such, he cannot sincerely be our friend. An American is the born enemy of all European peoples."[75]

In December 1796, as Congress reconvened, the Republicans and Federalists were still at odds over which European nation was the most inimical to American interests, while the British still caused more damage to American shipping and sailors, the depredations of the French were beginning to surpass those of England. Noah Webster pointed to the reason, stating that no agent of the British government had "dared to foment sedition in our peaceful land by turning the American people against their government, as Genet, Fauchet, and Adet had done. Such bold insults are practiced by our *generous allies* [the French]. It is right; it is necessary that the insidious designs of such *sly, intriguing,* but *ambitious* and *domineering allies,* should be unmasked. They are more dangerous than armies of foes."[76]

As the Washington administration came to a close, the French began to openly treat American commerce as they did British commerce, including confiscation of American vessels, and the arrest and execution of American seamen as pirates, in the hope that these actions would insure a Republican president in the upcoming election. It was not to be however for on February 8, 1797, a Federalist, John Adams was elected to the American presidency.[77]

---

75   Dumas Malone, *Ordeal of Liberty*, p. 290

76   Alexander DeConde, *Entangling Alliances*, p. 488

77   Harlow Giles Unger, *The French War Against America: How a Trusted Ally Betrayed Washington and the Founding Fathers* (Hoboken, NJ: John Wiley & Sons Inc., 2005), p. 177-191

Chapter 3

John Adams Becomes President

My entrance into office is marked by a misunderstanding with France, which I shall endeavor to reconcile, provided that no violation of faith, no stain upon honor, is exacted. But if infidelity, dishonor, or too much humiliation is demanded, France shall do as she pleases, and take her course. America is not SCARED.[1]

John Adams wrote these words in March, 1797, upon taking office as the second president of the United States. In November, he wrote to his wife Abigail, "If I have looked with any accuracy into the hearts of my fellow citizens, the French will find as the English have found, that feelings may be stirred which they never expected to find there, and that perhaps, the American people themselves are not sensible are within them."[2]

The French were only one of Adam's concerns as he began his presidency, the other major problem was politics, which would also have a bearing on his handling of foreign affairs. The Founding Fathers realized that there would be opposition within the American political system, but the rejected political parties as being evil and dangerous to the common good, this rejection however led to confusion and tension during the early American republic. The

---

1   Jonathan M. Neilson, *Paths Not Taken* (Westport, Connecticut: Praeger, 2000), p. 14

2   John Adams to Abagail Adams, November 27, 1796

presidential election of 1796 was an example of this tension because for the first time, the nation could not unite behind a hero such as George Washington.

Not only did the America democracy produce what the Fathers feared, political parties, but also divisions between the parties, especially within the Federalist Party. Both Alexander Hamilton and John Adams were highly influential during the Washington administration; Adams as Vice President and Hamilton as Secretary of the Treasury. Now, in 1797, Hamilton represented the High Federalists[3] and Adams the moderate Federalists. This division in the Federalist Party began to take shape following a tense negotiation between Adams, Washington, and the High Federalists over the rankings of appointments in the army. Adams was humiliated in this episode where the former president insisted that Hamilton (who had the title general during the Revolution) serve as second in command of the army, overriding Adam's preference to preserve the rankings in place from the Revolutionary War (those rankings would have placed Hamilton third, behind Henry Knox and Charles Pinckney). With Hamilton second in command to an aging Washington, meant to Adams that in the event of war with France, Hamilton would command the army. Also the High Federalists hoped to build the new Republic's military capacity. Many Federalists viewed these two objects as cut from the same cloth.[4]

At first, the views of John Adams and Alexander Hamilton on the potential conflict with France were very similar, the main issue between them was actually party politics. Hamilton believed in the existence of only one party, an entity that had as its main objective

---

3   The High Federalists shared the same beliefs as the Federalist Party in general: principally, the desire for a national bank and maintaining a strong central government. The major difference was that the High Federalists believed in going to war with France, a belief that separated them from John Adams' more moderate wing of the party. This split had an impact on the election of 1800, leading to the election of Thomas Jefferson, a Democrat-Republican.

4   Jeffrey S. Selinger, "Making Sense of Presidential Restraint: Federalist Arrangements and Executive Decision Making Before the Civil War", *Presidential Studies Quarterly*, February 14, 2014

the defeat of the nation's enemies. Adams, on the other hand did not believe that political parties should exist at all, and therefore, wished to remain above their influence, joining the framers. Richard Hofstader in his work *The Idea of a Party System* lays out the basic ideology of political actors in the early Republic with regard to parties. The framers and early American politicians were and continued to be against parties or factions for almost all of their lives.[5] While all agreed in the principle of opposition, they were not sure in what form this opposition would take. They saw factions as dangerous, and instead preferred public officials to use "disinterested good judgment on behalf of the public welfare" and be an individual "free from [the] distortions of judgment."[6] The founders' distrust of parties came from two sources; historical precedent in England and philosophers who wrote on the subject such as Henry of Bollingbroke and David Hume. For the founders, "party was associated with painfully deep and unbridgeable differences in national politics. . . .with treason and the threat of foreign invasion, with instability and dangers to liberty."[7]

Not only did Adams have to deal with this attitude among the political elite in the nation, and the fact that the parties did exist with very real differences, but also the divisions within his own party, led by Hamilton who continually attempted to control Adams as he did other members of the Federalist Party.

The major "very real difference" and an extremely volatile one centered on the attitude of the two political groups, the Federalists and the Democratic-Republicans towards France. As an example, Hamilton referred to Jefferson and the Republicans as "Jacobins," under the control of the French government.[8] The goal of the

---

5   Richard Hofstadter, *The Idea of a Party System: The Rise of Legitimate Opposition in the United States,* 1780-1840 (Berkley: University of California Press, 1969), p. 11

6   *Ibid.,* p. 13

7   *Ibid.,* p. 12

8   Harold C. Syrett, *The Papers of Alexander Hamilton, Volume XXI* (New York:

"Jacobins," according to Hamilton, was to create "a *new model* [for] our constitution under the *influence* and *coercion* of France" and make America, essentially a "province of France."[9] On the other hand, Hamilton saw the Federalists as true Americans. He believed that "there is in this country a decided French Faction, but no other foreign faction."[10] Unlike Hamilton, Adams saw the existence of a British faction in American politics. During his 1796 campaign for President, Adams wrote that "the English Party have outgeneraled the French and American both."[11] The agreement between Hamilton and Adams was in the fact that they both saw themselves above foreign influence and private ambitions, however, since according to Hamilton the French (Republican) Party existed, he could justify his behavior as noble and unselfish in purpose. Similarly, Adams believed that he was a true member of the "American" Party, and therefore his interests lied solely in the best interests of the American people.

Adams however was the loser in his positioning as an "American." He had the Republicans on one side and the High Federalists on the other. Even though as early as 1787, when he saw the beginnings of the political parties, he believed that they could be controlled. "the great desideratum in a government is a distinct executive power of sufficient strength and weight to compel [parties] to submit to laws."[12] As president however, Adams realized that he would not gain the control that he sought. The Republicans gave him little support as a Federalist, and the High Federalists denounced him when he tried to exert his independence.

The first signs of the enmity between Hamilton and Adams

Columbia University Press, 1974), p. 81

9   *Ibid.*, p. 467

10 *Ibid.* p. 452

11 John Adams to Abigail Adams, December 16, 1796. This was a reference to the fact that the Federalists convinced the South not to give Adams any Electoral College votes.

12 Stephen G. Kurtz, "The French Mission of 1799-1800," *The Academy of Political Science*, 80, no. 4 (Dec., 1965), p. 546

occurred during the 1796 presidential election and would have a direct bearing on American relations with the French. Historians of this period in American history have diverse opinions on Hamilton's actions toward the election. Stanley Elkins argues that there is "little doubt that what Hamilton really wanted was to get Adams out of the way altogether. . . .and ease in the more tractable [Charles] Pinckney as President."[13]While this is the majority viewpoint, another possibility comes from John Harper. He argues that rather than attempting to deprive Adams of the Presidency, Hamilton's main focus was to ensure that Jefferson with his views on France, would become President. In a letter to a friend, Hamilton is quoted as stating that "the exclusion of Jefferson is far more important than any difference between Mr. Adams and Mr. Pinckney."[14]

Regardless of Hamilton's machinations, Adams took office in 1797, with two major problems; a growing division within the Federalist Party, which would impact on the other difficulty, international relations (basically with France). Realizing this, coupled with his doubts, he wrote to Abigail in December of 1796 "the Election is a Lott at this hour and if my Reason were to dictate I should wish to be left out. A. P[resident] with half a Continent upon his Back besides all France and England old Tories and all Jacobins to carry will have a devilish Load. He will be very apt to Stagger and stumble."[15]In the same month, he wrote to his wife on another aspect of international relations, American neutrality towards England and France created by George Washington "[I] must be an intrepid to encounter the open assaults of France and the Secret Plotts of England, in concert with all his treacherous Friends and open Enemies in his own country."

Adam's position with regards to France upon taking office was

13 Stanley Elkins, *The Age of Federalism* (New York: Oxford University Press, 1993), p. 524

14 John Harper, *American Machiavelli* (New York: Cambridge University Press, 2004), p. 196

15 John Adams to Abagail Adams, December 7, 1796

very straightforward, he would pursue every peaceful means to reach a reconciliation with France, but he would not compromise America's honor or dignity in the process. In his private letters, he reiterated his determination to keep peace with France while also remaining neutral in her conflict with England. "I dread not a War, with France or England, if either forces it upon Us, but *will make no aggression upon either*, with my free Will, without just and necessary Cause and Provocation."[16] Interestingly, there was a dichotomy between Adam's wish to get along with the French and his affection for them. Writing to Abigail at the beginning of January, 1797, he stated that he would "Support the course taken of the United States, *and the system of impartial Neutrality* but if belligerent Powers, until it should be otherwise ordained by Congress – consistent with that Duties I shall always be *friendly to the French*."[17] At the end of the same month, again writing to his wife, Adams said that he believed that America had been "insulted by France," and that these insults had divided America, and also that the "French have plundered and wronged Us twice as much as the English."[18] Much of his opinion of the French came from the time when he served as ambassador to France during the Revolution. And finally, as a true Federalist, he asserted, again to his wife, "The French character whether under Monarchical or Republican Government is not the most equitable, nor the least assuring of all Nations. The Fire, Impetuosity, and Vehemence of their Consit Temperament is apt to be violent, immoderate and extravagant. The Passions are always outrageous. A Frenchman in Love, must shoot himself or succeed. A Frenchman in Anger must shed the Blood of his Object, and so of the rest."[19]

The French were well aware of Adam's viewpoints, and responded to his election with an order to treat American ships as enemy vessels. The American consul at Algiers, Joel Barlow wrote

---

16 *Ibid.*, November 27, 1796

17 *Ibid.*, January 3, 1797

18 *Ibid.*, January 31, 1797

19 *Ibid.*, December 4, 1796

from France shortly after the election that "the French saw that the character of the new President would be a criterion by which the friendship or enmity of the United States for France could clearly be seen. . . . when the election of Adams was announced here it produced the order [to treat American vessels as enemy ships], which was meant to be little short of a declaration of war."[20]

To formulate a plan to deal with the French, Adams solicited opinions from his cabinet. Secretary of War, James McHenry asked Hamilton for his views on the subject. Hamilton's reply showed that he was in agreement with Adams as to the course America should take. On April 7, 1797, in a letter to William Loughton Smith, the Federalist chairman of the House Committee on Ways and Means, Hamilton wrote that "I would disarm them of all pleas that we have not made every possible effort for peace."[21] A few days later he again wrote to Smith that "my idea is another attempt to pacify by negotiation."[22] In this, Hamilton and Adams were in agreement, no peace at the expense of honor. Hamilton was "disposed to make no sacrifices to France. [He] had rather perish [himself] and family than see the country disgraced."[23] Additionally, he advocated that America "do everything that *honor permits* toward accommodation."[24]

While both men agreed on a course of action with respect to France, they had different motivations for their beliefs. Adams never enunciated any specific reason for maintaining peace with France. Hamilton however did. He wished to keep peace with France in order to keep the "Jacobin criticism" silent and unite the American people. Hamilton argued that the American government should "keep in view as a primary objective union at home"[25] and to "unite the

---

20 Frank Donavon, *The John Adam's Papers* (New York: Dodd Mead & Company, 1965), p. 254

21 Harold Syrett, *The Papers of Alexander Hamilton*, Volume XXI, p. 21

22 *Ibid.*, p. 26

23 *Ibid.*, p. 21

24 *Ibid.*, p. 26

25 *Ibid.*, p. 22

opinions of all good Citizens of whatever political denomination"[26] behind any action the government ended up taking.

Like Washington and other Federalist leaders, Adams never doubted that France was wrong and that the United States was right, but unlike many of the leaders of his own party, he wished to resolve the conflict through diplomacy.

As a politician, Hamilton joined Adams in the hope that diplomacy would end the current problems with France because if the United States went to war with France, the Federalists might find themselves leaders of a disunited country at a time when they would need the confidence and resources of all the people. In addition, Hamilton believed that a main objective of the nation's foreign policy was to rid itself of the entangling French alliance of 1778. While the alliance was practically dead after the Jay Treaty and Washington's Proclamation of Neutrality, a special diplomatic mission to France might end the alliance and might also avert a war.

Hamilton also believed that with the change in the nation's administration, the French might be willing to negotiate without losing face, as it might have if it were still dealing with the previous administration. In a letter to Theodore Sedgwick, the Speaker of the House, Hamilton gave his ideas on the mission to France, "Were I Mr. Adams, then I believe I should begin my Presidency by naming an extraordinary commission to the French Republic, and perhaps . . . abrogate or remodify the treaty of alliance. "He believed that the commission should explain American policy, remonstrate against French actions, and seek indemnities for spoliations of America shipping while negotiating a new commercial treaty.[27]

The Republicans also agreed with the idea of a special mission to France, pointing out the fact that in 1794 such a mission was sent to England resulting in the Jay Treaty, and now another mission could prevent war with the French. As the day for Adam's inauguration

---

26 *Ibid.*, p. 21

27 Alexander Hamilton to Theodore Sedgwick, February 26, 1797

approached, the idea of such a mission had become a popular topic of discussion, even in the newspapers.

Adams desired nation unity and believed that this commission to the France could serve two purposes, first, if he set up the commission to include both Federalists and Republicans, it would be taken seriously by the French, secondly, that a bi-partisan commission would show a foreign policy of neutrality, and finally that he hoped to gain Republican support for his administration. Vice President Jefferson and the Republicans were willing to offer such support and to go along with the President-elects plan because they were anxious to keep the new administration from falling under control of extremists who appeared bent on war with France.[28]

Jefferson was convinced that he could work effectively with Adams, especially in the realm of foreign affairs. He believed that Adams did not want war with France, and even though he was a Federalist and had sympathy for England, would not truckle to the British. Jefferson had also written a friendly letter to Adams offering cooperation, and although the letter was never sent, its substance reached Adams convincing him that there was an opportunity to bury past differences and possibly gain Jefferson's support.

There was some alarm among the Federalists at this possible reconciliation between Adams and Jefferson, but Hamilton was not worried, "Our Jacobins say they are well pleased and that the lion and the lamb are to lie down together. Mr. Adams PERSONAL friends talk a little in the same way." Yet he explained, Adams had a basic loyalty to the Federalist system and hence the *rapprochement* with Jefferson could not last.[29]

The problem that Adams now faced was who to send to France as members of this commission. Initially, Adams' idea was to send three representatives to France; Charles Cotesworth Pinckney, who

---

28 Nathan Schachner, *The Founding Fathers* (New York: A.S. Barnes & Company, Inc., 1954), p. 417

29 Alexander Hamilton to Rufus King, February 15, 1797

was already in France and was a staunch Federalist, James Madison, who shared the leadership of the Republican Party with Jefferson, and Elbridge Gerry, a friend of Adams from Massachusetts who was a lukewarm Federalist with Republican leanings.

Problems with his commission selections began immediately, first with Madison. The Presidents first consultation was with his cabinet, who were mainly Federalists. Oliver Wolcott, the Secretary of the Treasury, said of Madison as a member of the group, "will make dire work among the passions of our parties in Congress, and out of doors thro' the States," and even offered to resign. Adams then decided to consult other advisers and party leaders among them George Washington. He discovered that Federalist opposition to Madison was so intense as to endanger confirmation of the mission in the Senate. Rather than risk open turmoil in his party Adams decided to exclude Madison and to postpone a decision on the mission itself, but he did not make this decision public.[30] In March of 1797, Adams was told by Jefferson that Madison could not go to France. After this, Adams did not consult his Vice President on matters of policy, thus ending the possibility of true cooperation between the President and the Republican leaders.[31] Added to the problem of losing Madison, Adams learned that the French had refused to accept Pinckney sent to replace Madison by George Washington.

Also in March, the French Directory issued a decree that completely violated the Franco-American Treaty of 1787, by annulling the principle of free ships, free goods. Now, the French could capture neutral vessels carrying British goods. Additionally, any American found serving under an enemy flag would be considered a pirate, and all American ships that did not carry a list of crew and passengers would be considered a lawful prize.[32]

---

30 Alexander DeConde, *The Quasi-War: The Politics and Diplomacy of the Undeclared War with France 1797-1801* (New York: Charles Scribner's Sons, 1966), p. 15

31 Manning J. Dauer, *The Adams Federalists* (Baltimore: John Hopkins University Press, 1993), p. 125

32 Rufus King Papers, Huntington Library, San Marino, California

Given the situation, Adams had three choices; he could ask Congress for an embargo on American shipping, mainly on cargoes destined for the Caribbean and French ports, he could ask the Congress for a declaration of war against France, or he could continue his present course of avoiding war without surrendering the nation's honor. His decision was to continue to put together a special mission while at the same time strengthening the national defense. While Jefferson remained skeptical about continuing with the special mission plan, the bulk of the Federalists, including Hamilton supported the idea, coupled with measures for defense. Specifically, they advised him to arm merchant and to create a naval force capable of providing convoy escorts to protect the ships. In general, the majority of both parties recommended that Adams should make an effort to reach an agreement with France comparable to Jay's Treaty, but at the same time prepare for the worst.

After trying roiling debate, Congress approved an Act Providing a Naval Armament on July 1, 1797. The act funded the building, equipping and manning of the warships *Constitution, United States, and the Constellation,* and provided some money for harbor forts, but nothing more.

In addition to having the warships built, Adams also chided the French government saying that its refusal to accept one of the American diplomats "until we have acceded to their demands without discussion and without investigation, is to treat us neither as allies, nor as friends, nor as a sovereign State."[33] On the same subject, he continued accusing France of attempting to "separate the people of the United States from the government" and vowed that America would show with their response that "we are not a degraded people. . . .fitted to be miserable instruments of foreign influence, and regardless of national honor, character, and interest."[34]

In October 1797, Adams put together the components of

33 Frank Donavon, *The John Adams Papers,* p. 255

34 *Ibid.* p. 256

the mission to France. It was composed of Charles Pinckney and Elbridge Gerry, but instead of James Madison, he sent John Marshall. The group met with Charles Maurice deTalleyrand who was now the French foreign minister on their arrival. Talleyrand informed his American guests that he was writing a report for the Directory on United States policy and preferred to postpone negotiations until he had completed it and gained the Directory's approval of its recommendations.[35] In his place the commission was directed to meet with three French officials who informed them that for the negotiations to go forward, the French would need "an apology for disparaging remarks Adams made about France in his recent message to Congress, a payment of $250,000 and a loan of $12 million."[36]

Although they would later claim moral outrage, Pinckney, Marshall, and Gerry knew that bribery was common in European diplomacy. They refused to pay the bribe not out of moral outrage, but out of political practicality – they had no money to pay the bribe and also had no guarantees that if they paid it the negotiations would go forward.[37] More important any loan to France would have violated America's neutrality in the French war with Britain and could have potentially caused a war between Britain and the United States.[38]

This episode is the genesis of what became known as the X Y Z Affair, so called because when news of the commission's problems in dealing with the French became known, President Adams replaced the names of the French negotiators with the letters W X Y and Z. In the actual negotiations, on October 17, 1797, Nicholas Hubbard, an Englishman working for a Dutch bank used by the Americans (and who came to be identified as ("W") in the published papers), notified Pinckney that Baron Jean-Conrad Hottinguer, a French banker, whom Hubbard identified only as a man of honor, wished to

---

35 Thomas Pickering Papers (Massachusetts Historical Society)

36 Howard Jones, *The Course of American Democracy* (Danbury: Scholastic Library Publishing, 1985), p. 35

37 Jonathan M. Neilson, *Paths Not Taken* (Westport: Praeger, 2000), p. 15

38 Howard Jones, *The Course of American Democracy*, p. 35

meet with him. Pinckney agreed. In the meeting Hottinguer (who was later identified as ("X") again brought up the subject of the bribes, but also asked for a 50,000 pound payment to Talleyrand. Hottinguer then introduced the commission to Pierre Bellamy ("Y"), who he represented as being a member of Talleyrand's inner circle.[39] Bellamy expounded in detail on Talleyrand's demands, including the expectation that *"you must pay a great deal of money."*[40]He even suggested a series of purchases (at inflated prices) of currency as a means by which such money could be clandestinely exchanged.[41]At this point, the American commissioners offered to send one of their number back to the United States for instructions, if the French would suspend their seizures of American shipping, the French negotiators refused.[42]

Shortly after the standoff, Talleyrand sent Lucien Hauteval, a wealthy planter from Santo Domingo who was known to be friendly to the United States ("Z") to meet with Elbridge Gerry. The two men knew each other, having met in Boston in 1792. Hauteval assured Gerry of Talleyrand's sincerity in seeking peace, and encouraged him to keep the informal negotiations open, while at the same time reiterating the demands for a loan and a bribe.[43]

A week later, Hottinger and Bellamy again met with the commission and repeated their original demands, this time accompanied by threats of potential war.[44] Pinckney's response to the

---

39 William Stinchcombe, "The Diplomacy of the WXYZ Affair" *William and Mary Quarterly* (34): p. 599

40 George Billias, *Elbridge Gerry, Founding Father and Republican Statesman* (Columbus: McGraw-Hill, 1976), p. 270

41 William Stinchcombe, "The Diplomacy of the WXYZ Affair. P. 599

42 *Ibid.*

43 *Ibid.*

44 The French believed that they could make this threat because they had just signed the Treaty of Compo Formio ending the War of the First Coalition between France and most of the other European powers.

French was: "No, no, not a sixpence!"[45] With this the commissioners decided on November 1, 1797 to refuse further negotiations through informal channels. Publication of their dispatches describing this series would form the basis for later political debates in the United States.[46]

In late November Talleyrand finally appeared at a dinner primarily to castigate the Americans for their unwillingness to accede to the demands for a bribe. When this had no effect, he then began to attempt to cause a rift among the Commission by inviting Gerry to a "social" dinner without the other two, believing that he would be the easiest to sway to the French point of view. Gerry attended seeking to maintain communications, however this action resulted in a distrust of Gerry by Marshall and Pinckney.

While these private negotiations between both sides now became the norm, the division between Gerry on one side and Marshall and Pinckney on the other continued to grow to the point that Talleyrand began to increase the pressure by telling Gerry in January 1798 that he would no longer deal with Pinckney. In February, he also excluded Marshall. Next Gerry, at Talleyrand's insistence, began keeping secret from the other commissioners the substance of their meetings.[47]

By March of 1798, it was clear that the negotiations were at an impasse, even though Talleyrand dropped the demand for a loan. Additionally, Talleyrand would still only communicate with Gerry. In April, Marshall and Pinckney left France for the United States, Gerry remained behind after being told by Talleyrand that if he left Paris, The French would declare war on the United States.[48]He remained optimistic that war was unrealistic, writing to William Vans Murray, the American ambassador to the Netherlands that "nothing but

---

45 William Stinchcombe, "The Diplomacy of the WXYZ Affair." P. 600

46 *Ibid.*

47 George Billias, *Elbridge Gerry, Founding Father and Republican Statesman*, p. 275

48 Ibid., p. 280

madness" would cause the French to declare war.[49]

By the end of March, the results of the negotiations began to become known in the United States. The Republicans believed that France would not declare war against the United States and that they, the French, really wanted to continue the talks, and so wished the negotiations to become public. The extreme Federalists believing that the treatment of the commissioners by the French would damage the Republicans, also wanted them to become public.

President Adams, stole a march on both groups by sending all the dispatches to the House of Representatives on April 3, telling the Congress what the consequence would be if the documents were made public.[50] When the House Republicans examined the correspondence, they were astounded, recognizing immediately that public disclosure would arouse the citizenry to such an extent that it would precipitate the very war that they wished to prevent. After much discussion however the House voted to make the negotiations public. Three days later, the Senate, where the documents were also examined voted to make their contents public.

When news reached the public in the United States about the happenings in Paris specifically the insults generated by Talleyrand, war sentiment became very high. As an example, "numerous Quakers set aside their pacifist beliefs and called for honor at the cost of war."[51] In Philadelphia, there seemed to be no doubt about the reaction. "the public opinion," Abigail Adams observed, "is changing here very fast, and the people begin to see who have been their firm unshaken friends, steady to their interests and defenders of their Rights and Liberties." After all, she pointed out, "the olive Branch, tended to our Gallic Allies, by our Envoys; has been rejected with scorn."[52] The

---

49 Ibid., p. 281

50 Adams to Congress, April 3, 1798

51 Howard Jones, *The Course of American Democracy*, p. 37

52 Alexander DeConde, *The Quasi-War: The Politics and Diplomacy of the Undeclared War With France*, 1797-1801, p. 75

tricolor cockade of France that many, mostly Republicans, had been wearing recently now practically disappeared. Those who still dared to flaunt the cockades ran the risk of being mobbed and having the tricolor torn from their hats. More significantly, many Republicans began to support a war with France as well. Twenty-one years after the American people looked upon France as their greatest ally when they declared their independence, were now ready to make war on perhaps the nation that did the most to support that independence.

All during this international crisis, Hamilton had been writing essays in the press to warn people of the danger they faced from France. Through April he wrote a series of articles called the "Stand" in which he outlined his program calling for; arsenals, an army, a navy, the licensing of privateers, the borrowing in anticipation of new tax revenues, and the suspension of the alliance and other treaties with France by an act of Congress. The High Federalists welcomed the war crisis which they believed could be used to regain power. Attempting to equate the Federalist program with patriotism to make them appear synonymous, one Federalist journal stated, "To be lukewarm after reading the horrid scenes (in the X Y Z letters) is to be criminal-and the man who does not warmly reprobate the conduct of the French must have a soul black enough to be *fit* for *treasons stratagems* and *spoils*."[53] The main exception to this outlook was the Federalist leader, Alexander Hamilton, who according to the historian Stanley Elkin's view, "the advice Adams received from Hamilton . . . might have been the most rational of any."[54] Hamilton, before news of the French refusal of the American delegates, advised Adams through James McHenry, the Secretary of War that even if the new mission to France failed, that "there is a strong aversion to War in the minds of the people . . . by a formal war with France there is nothing to be gained." He advised instead that "a truly vigorous defensive plan, with the countenance of a readiness to negotiate, is the course advisable to be pursued."[55]

---

53 The New York *Gazette*, April 12, 1798

54 Stanley Elkins, *The Age of Federalism*, p. 584

55 Harold C. Syrett, *The Papers of Alexander Hamilton, Volume XXI*, p. 342

There is a great deal of circumstantial evidence to suggest that Hamilton may have wanted a declaration of war with France; his past disagreements with Adams, his eventual change of heart on this issue, his dislike of the French and his position as unofficial leader of the High Federalists all suggest that he wished for a conflict with France, however there is no direct evidence to support this contention until months after the X Y Z Affair.

Adams, on the other hand was initially quite belligerent after learning of the poor treatment of the American diplomats by the French. Possibly, the reason for this stance was the new popularity that he gained by catering to the public's war sentiment. As an example, the president, wearing full military garb would declare "the finger of destiny writes on the wall the word: War"[56] and speaking to an audience, "to arms, then, my young friends,"[57] In the end however, he would decide against sending a declaration of war to Congress.

There seemed to be only one aspect of foreign policy that the majority of both the Republicans and the Federalists agreed upon and that was that the nation was in peril, but for different reasons. The Republicans argued that the danger lay in the Federalist desire for war, and the Federalists that the problem lay in France's aggressive policy towards the United States.

By June of 1798, fear of invasion by the French through the southern states enhanced the desire of the Federalists to cooperate with Great Britain. Some High Federalists even suggested that this cooperation become a military alliance, the United States would take Louisiana and the Floridas, and Britain would seize Santo Domingo. Henry Knox, Washington's Secretary of War told Adams that "indeed we are vulnerable in the Southern States to an alarming degree. The British navy is the only preventive against an invasion of these States from the West India Island."[58]

---

56 Jonathon M. Neilson, *Paths Not Taken*, p. 17

57 Frank Donavon, *The John Adam's Papers*, p. 265

58 Henry Knox to John Adams, June 26, 1798

The other concern that the Federalists had with the South was its political control by the Republican Party. To dissipate the party's strength, Hamilton suggested to George Washington that he take a trip through the South ostensibly for reasons of health, but in fact to stimulate demonstrations of loyalty to the government. While Washington refused, in June, writing to Hamilton, he stated, "if the French should be so mad as openly and formidably to invade these United States, in expectation of subjugating the government, laying them under contribution, or in hopes of dissolving the Union, I conceive there can hardly be two opinions respecting their Plan, and their operations will commence in the Southern quarter."[59]

The war sentiment began to be translated into government action. During the summer of 1798, "several steps toward war short of a formal declaration" were enacted by Congress with the support of President Adams. Even though his cabinet was divided on how to react: the general tenor was one of hostility toward France. This hostility received was augmented when Pierre Bellamy ("Y") of the X Y Z Affair boasted that "the Diplomatic skill of France and the means she possess in your country, are sufficient to enable her, with the French party in America, to throw the blame which will attend the rupture of the of the negotiations on the Federalist, as you term yourselves, but on the British party, as France terms you. "This boast was to cause suspicion and wide spread denunciation of the Republican Party and its leaders. Senator Theodore Sedgwick, the Federalist majority whip, after hearing of the X Y Z Affair, opined "It will afford a glorious opportunity to destroy faction. Improve it." Hamilton equated the public's perception of the Republican opposition to the Federalist's agenda like that of the Tories in the Revolution. It is quite possible that this boast by Bellamy began the process that would eventually cause the Alien and Sedition Acts of 1798.[60]

The Federalist majority in Congress passed the four laws whose purpose was to make the United States more secure from foreign

59 George Washington to Alexander Hamilton, May 27, 1798

60 http://schoolworkhelper.net/the -sedition-act-of-1798-summary-analysis

spies and domestic traitors, but also to weaken Jefferson's Republican Party.

The first law, the Naturalization Act (June 13, 1798) extended the time that immigrants had to live in the United States to become citizens from five to fourteen years. Since most immigrants favored the Republicans, delaying their citizenship would inhibit the growth of Jefferson's party.

The Alien Enemies Act (June 22, 1798) stated that once war was declared, all male citizens of an enemy nation could be arrested, detained, and deported. If war had broken out, this act could have expelled the estimated 25,000 French citizens then living in the United States. The war was never used since the conflict with France was not declared.

The Alien Friends Act (July 6, 1798) authorized the president to deport any non-citizen suspected of plotting against the government during either peacetime or wartime. This law could have resulted in the mass expulsion of new immigrants. Its term was two years, but no alien was ever deported under it.

The fourth law was the Sedition Act. Its provisions seemed to be directly aimed at anyone who spoke out against the Federalists. The basis of the act came from English common law, there "seditious libel" prohibited virtually any criticism of the king or his officials, because to criticize either undermined the respect of the people for their authority.

In the United States, the Sedition Act outlawed conspiracies "to oppose any measure or measures of the government. "Additionally, the act made it illegal for anyone to express "any false, scandalous and malicious writing" against Congress or the president.[61]

The connection to English law by the Federalists was important because they could argue that freedom of speech and the press only

---

61 Significantly, the act did not include the vice-president who of course was Thomas Jefferson.

applied before the expression of ideas. The government could not censor or stop someone from expressing ideas until after the words had been spoken or printed if they had maliciously defamed the king or his government. While the Republicans simply contended that the Sedition Law violated the First Amendment to the Constitution. After being enacted, the law was set to expire on March 3, 1801, the last day of President Adam's term.

With the power given to them by the Alien and Sedition Acts, the Federalists began to use it to their advantage. Fourteen indictments were brought under the Sedition Acts, mostly against editors and publishers of Republican newspapers. The indictments forced many Republican newspapers to close down and intimidated others into ceasing any criticism of the federal governments.

The most celebrated of these cases concerned a Vermont Republican congressman, Matthew Lyon, who wrote a letter published in his own newspaper *The Scourge of Aristocracy and Repository of Important Political Truth* on October 1, 1798, criticizing President Adams for his "unbounded thirst for ridiculous pomp, foolish adulation, and selfish avarice." As well as Adams' corruption of religion to further his war aims.[62]

A federal grand jury indicted Lyon for intentionally stirring up hatred against President Adams. During the trial, Lyon attempted to prove the truth of what he had said and written, as permitted by the Sedition Act. This meant that the burden of proof was on him, he had to prove that what he said and wrote was true, not that the prosecutor had to prove them false. The jury found Lyon guilty, sentencing him to four months in jail, a $1000 fine, and court costs. Lyon ran for re-election to Congress from his jail cell and won, his Vermont supporters welcomed him as a hero.

The Republicans had public opinion against them for their support of the French and now added to that situation, political

---

62 Claude Gernade, *Jefferson and Hamilton: The Struggle for Democracy in America* (Boston: Houghton Mifflin, 1925) p. 386

control of the government by the Federalists, who had just passed the Alien and Sedition Acts. To counter the Federalists legally, the Republicans attempted to have the acts declared unconstitutional. The question was how to challenge the acts without having those individuals who challenged them accused of violating them.

The states of Kentucky and Virginia were used as venues by Thomas Jefferson and James Madison to attack the acts. Both Republicans wrote separate statements that were issued by the two states legislatures. Thomas Jefferson drafted the Kentucky Resolutions which was passed by the Kentucky House of Representatives in November 1798. The Virginia Resolutions were introduced by James Madison which were passed by the Virginia House of Delegates in December 1798. At the times of their passage authorship of both document were known only to a few close associates because either author could have been charged with sedition because they were charging that the Alien and Sedition Acts were unconstitutional. The fact that Jefferson was vice president would not have saved him from prosecution.

Because of the need for secrecy, no written records have surfaced detailing the work done by Jefferson and Madison in putting together their resolutions. During November of 1798 however Jefferson sent a draft of his resolution to Madison along with a letter stating "I think we should distinctly affirm all the important principles they contain so as to hold to that ground in future."[63]

The two documents when presented were clearly different from one another. Jefferson's resolution was more forceful that Madison's, stating that when the federal government "assumes undelegated powers, its acts are unauthoritative, void, and of no force."[64] Madison's Virginia Resolutions were more temperate. They asserted that the states were "duty bound, to impose" whenever the federal government assumed "a deliberate, palpable and dangerous

---

63 Jefferson to Madison, November 17, 1798

64 Papers of Thomas Jefferson, 30:547

exercise" of powers not granted by the Constitution.[65] Madison did not chose the form of interposition. Rather he purposely used "general expressions" allowing the other states to consider "all the modes possible" for concurring with Virginia.[66]

Unfortunately for Jefferson and Madison, no other states joined in either of the resolutions, ten states even expressed disapproval. Some pointed out the judiciary, not the state legislatures, were responsible for determining questions of constitutionality. In response to this criticism both states passed new resolutions, Kentucky in 1799, and Virginia in 1800. Kentucky's new resolution went further than its predecessor, asserting that "the several states who formed [the Constitution]. . . .have the unquestionable right to judge of its infraction; and, That a nullification . . . of all unauthorized acts . . . is the rightful remedy."[67] Though the other states rejected the Kentucky and Virginia Resolutions, the measures served effectively as political propaganda and helped to unite the Republican Party.[68]

At the same time that the Republican Party was having problems in fighting the Alien and Sedition Acts, the president while still retaining the position of armed neutrality began to look at the possibility of sending another delegation to France. In a message to Congress on this topic, he stated "but to send another minister without more determinate assurances that he would be received, would be an act of humiliation to which the United States ought not to submit. It must, therefore, be left to France, if she is indeed desirous of accommodation, to take the requisite steps."[69] In possibly reopening the door to a peaceful reconciliation with France, Adams was also beginning to move away from Hamilton who had begun to believe that a war with France was becoming likely.

---

65 Papers of James Madison, 17:189

66 Madison to Jefferson, December 29, 1798

67 Kentucky Resolutions of 1799, December 3, 1799

68 Adrienne Koch and Harry Ammon, "The Virginia and Kentucky Resolutions: An Episode in Jefferson's and Madison's Defense of Civil Liberties," *William & Mary Quarterly*, 3d ser., vol. 5, no.2 (April 1948), p. 147

69 Frank Donavon, *The John Adam's Papers*, p. 272

The president's opportunity came at the beginning of 1799 when Eldridge Gerry who had remained in France after the previous mission failed, wrote to Adams that France was willing to meet with America on respectful terms. As a result, without consulting his cabinet, Adams nominated William Vans Murray to be minister to France in February of 1799.

This announcement caused the final breakup between the Moderate and Hamiltonian Federalists. After the announcement Hamilton referred to the president as "a mere old woman and unfit for a President."[70] The decision did however cause consternation within the Federalist party in Congress, who were "graveled and divided; some for opposing, others know not what to do."[71]

70 *Ibid.* p. 272

71 *Ibid.*

Chapter 4

Commerce

While Jay's Treaty is given as the main reason of the Quasi War with France, based on diplomatic correspondence, there is another very important reason for the conflict – commerce. By mid-1796, the French government saw its commerce with the United States so badly disrupted that in their eyes the problem was the equal of the Jay Treaty.[1] Nearly every hope, plan, or policy France had entertained for her American trade partner had been disappointed or undone, either by events, such as the actions of the British or by the activities of American merchants and shipmasters attempting to profit from their neutral position between England and France.

With Britain's entry into the First Coalition,[2] French statesmen foresaw how important the United States would become, not as an active belligerent, but as a neutral carrier of foodstuffs.[3] Given the likelihood that Britain would interdict France's sea-borne commerce,

---

1 French Naval Records, series B and BB at the Archives Nationales de France (ANF)

2 Between 1793 and 1798, the First Coalition was formed to defeat the French. It was an alliance of: Spain, Holland, Austria, Prussia, England, and Sardinia.

3 Article 11 of the Treaty of Alliance between France and the United States stated that each country would help preserve the other's "liberty, Sovereignty, and Independence absolute, and unlimited, as well in Matters of Government as commerce." If the French had invoked this article, they would have gained a very weak ally, since the American military was in poor condition, better a strong trading partner.

and the resulting food shortages would renew the political unrest in Paris, they counted on the Americans to fill a vital supply role,[4] and to keep these supplies coming, they relied on the America's quest for profit. Additionally, the French also relied on American loyalty and goodwill, earned, the French believed, during the American struggle for independence from England. Unfortunately for the French, this assumptions were to undergo some dismaying vicissitudes.

In 1794, a large grain shipment totaling twenty four million pounds from the United States travelling in French ships safely reached France. The trip however was fraught with problems. The French convoy admiral, Pierre Van Stabel had to deal with the fact that his crews were crippled by an epidemic, that his departure was threatened by a congressional embargo, and a delay due to having to wait for the arrival of grain ships from such distant points as Charleston and New York. There was also the rumor that a British naval force was waiting to attack the convoy once it set sail. Van Stabel, however, in spite of the difficulties reached the French coast. Here however, the convoy came under attack by Lord Howe's fleet off Brest and was saved from destruction by the presence of French warships sent out to protect the convoy, allowing the grain ships to reach port. The French problem for the future was that in the ensuing battle with Howe, the French suffered the loss or disablement of the best part of their Atlantic navy.

With the almost complete destruction of this Atlantic fleet, protection for the grain convoys from the United States could not be repeated. Later during 1794, a smaller convoy was attacked by British Admiral Murray's squadron off Delaware Bay resulting in the capture of most of its ships. Within a year, French efforts to convoy their own vessels in the Atlantic were virtually abandoned. Thereafter, the arrival of American grain depended on the skill of individual shipmasters to elude what amounted to a blockade on both sides of the Atlantic.

---

4   For an explanation of the French food shortages, see Georges Lefebvre, *The Coming of the French Revolution* (New York, 1957), p. 90-94.

In 1795, with all of the grain reaching France arriving in American ships, the total volume was the highest of the decade in spite of the British renewing her previous year's practice of forcing grain ships into British ports. By 1796 however, Franco-American trade dropped off abruptly,[5] causing alarming food shortages. The two reasons for the decline were first that France did not rebuild their navy after the 1794 defeat at Brest. Within the year, April 1794 to April 1795, France's operational line vessels fell in number from 88 to 50 and her frigates from 128 to 64. Secondly, the French grain imports were subject to Britain's overwhelming mastery of the Atlantic Ocean.

This British mastery of the sea lanes extended to other waterways than the Atlantic. The French Naval Commissioner Jean Dalbarade reported that the English Channel was so thickly infested with British cruisers that merchantmen from Hamburg, Germany could penetrate no further towards France than Ostend, Belgian. To protect the expected grain ships from the United States, Dalbarade could do no more than station a small squadron off Brest. Otherwise, the navy was merely watching the coast to prevent "daily" landings of Englishmen and emigres (who were believed to be fomenting uprising in the nation). To that end, the navy had anchored "stationary" warships offshore and was using fishing boats for observation and patrol.[6]

Another French naval strategy in 1795, was to fill the Brest harbor with warships so that the British would have to set up an "invasion watch" using their Atlantic fleet. Should the British move their fleet, the French would then sail out of Brest, not to attack the English, but rather to compel them to return to Best, thereby keeping them out of the sea-lanes. Unfortunately for the French, the British

---

5   In 1795 the value of French imports from the United States was 75,171,584 francs, in 1796 it had dropped to 18,001,350 francs. See "A statement of the annual value of commerce between France and the United States during a period of twenty years from 1787 to 1806 inclusive," series F, doss. 501 ANF

6   Delbarade proposed similar strategies for the Channel coast and the Mediterranean.

had simply too many warships for the plan to work. In June, French Admiral Villaret-Joyeuse sailed from Brest to rescue a coastwise squadron that Admiral Howe had driven into the harbor on the island of Belle-Ile. Returning to port, Villaret-Joyeuse encountered a still larger force near the island of Groix. In what Dalbarade later described as "less an action than a rout," the British sent most of the Brest fleet scurrying into the harbor of Lorient, bloodied and demoralized.[7]

Despite the thin offshore cover provided by the French navy, large numbers of American ships still avoided capture or destruction. As late as July, American grain ships were crowding into Brest. While grain arrivals in the Atlantic were left largely to chance, alternate sources appeared briefly in the Mediterranean. In April, the French navy optimistically reported that there would be large increases in wheat shipments from Italy and North Africa, enough to feed not only Paris, but also southern France.[8] However, the plan depended on protecting the grain ships from attacks by British warships. To insure this, the French reinforced their fleet based in Toulon. In mid-July, this fleet was caught by a superior force under the command of British Admiral Hotham off the coast of the city of Hyeres and suffering severe losses, fled back to Toulon. Thereafter, massive desertions and a critical shortage of naval stores virtually ended French sea power in the Mediterranean for the remainder of the year. Inevitably, wheat imports suffered the consequences. By August, the French Supply Commission, reporting the enemy capture of 14 grain ships out of Genoa, concluded that the grain trade was widely disrupted.[9]

By mid-1795, it became clear that the French navy could not protect grain shipment coming by water from any direction. However, it was at this point that France began to import grain by land. French

---

7 Dalbarade to Comite de Salut public (Committee of Public Safety)

8 The navy's plan was to move grain across southwestern France via the Midi Canal which begins at the Etang de Thau (a lagoon on the Mediterranean) to Bordeaux via Toulouse on the Atlantic, a journey of 150 miles.

9 Report to the Committee of Public Safety, August 8, 1795

arms and French diplomacy allowed the nation to import grain from other Continental European nations. Military victories in Germany, Italy, and the Low Countries combined with Prussian and Spanish peace settlements assured the nation an adequate supply of foodstuffs. For French officials, 1795 was an instructive year. American grain, they knew, could furnish France the difference between shortage and sufficiency. But they also learned just how precarious was the reliance on overseas sources of grain.

More than the loss of the grain shipments, was the humiliation France felt by her reliance on American flag vessels to carry either in-or outbound cargoes. Whereas departing neutrals stood a fair chance of release after being detained by a British warship, French merchantmen escaped capture only when lucky.[10]In March of 1795, for example, a convoy of 40 French ships leaving Brest were attacked by British frigates losing 9 of its number, while 18 others were driven back to port. A worse example concerned Pierre Adet, who could not leave France for months to take up his position as ambassador to the United States because the French navy was extremely reluctant to send out single vessels, even an armed transport. After five months of delay, he finally set sail on the warship *Meduse*, but not before it was seriously suggested to him that he and his entourage be disguised as merchants, furnished with American passports, and sent by neutral vessel. By July, the French coast was under such heavy surveillance that the navy refused to move a corvette[11] from Brest to Rochefort, when asked to provide protection for the planned departure of "men and effects for India." The navy's explanation that the ship "would inevitably be intercepted, either as it left Brest, or at the mouth of the Channel, or in putting into Rochefort.[12]

---

10 Although Britain's right to seize enemy property from U.S. vessels was confirmed by Jay's Treaty, neutral owned cargoes departing from French ports were relatively safe. See Samuel F. Bemis, *Jay's Treaty, A Study in Commerceand Diplomacy*, (New Haven and London, 1962) p 335-336, 338

11 The smallest class of vessel considered to be a proper warship

12 Communication from the Commission de la Marine et des Colonies to the Comite de Salut public, July 28, 1795

The same situation obtained across the Atlantic. Compared with Van Stabel's massive convoy of 1794, French sailings out of U.S. ports were few and risky in 1795. Leaving the transport of grain entirely to American shipmasters, the French minister Joseph Fauchet consecrated on using the few armed cargo carriers (fluttes), France still had in American waters to export naval stores. In March three of these carriers successfully eluded a British squadron off Sandy Hook. Later that spring however three other fluttes ready to leave Norfolk were effectively blocked from sailing by a British force off Cape Henry. Ingress to American ports, moreover, was just as perilous as egress. Of five fluttes arriving from the Antilles in June, two were lost in a pitched battle with the British and the others so badly mauled as to be laid up in Norfolk for months of repair. Against such ravaging, Fauchet could do little more than send out a pilot boat to warn incoming vessels of the whereabouts of the British fleet.[13]

Even when commerce flourished, as it had in 1795 despite British interdictions, France encountered frustrations, now magnified by wartime conditions which pointed to a trade relationship with the United States long out of joint. Well before they singled out Jay's treaty as a principal cause of complaint, French officials had reached conclusions about Franco-American commerce, repeated so often in reports and analyses as to have become dishearteningly axiomatic.

First, was the fact that France had enjoyed a lively commerce with America during their war for independence, only to see American commerce return to the way it was before the war with England. Whatever the reason; French neglect, American ingratitude, or because British businessmen offered better terms, Anglo-American trade had risen from the ashes of Britain's defeat.[14] Secondly, not only did American traders return to doing business with the English, but

---

13 By late 1795, the navy agreed with the foreign office that French flag commerce in the U.S. had been reduced to a "nullity" by British cruisers. Commission de la Marine et des Colonies to the Commission des Relations Exterieures, December 23, 1795

14 A.C. Duplaine, "Notes on the Commerce of France with the United States of America," August, 1794

they also competed with the French in selling their own goods. In 1784, France opened three West Indies ports to trade, immediately American merchants moved in *en masse,* marketing slaves, cheap cottons and foodstuffs and taking away sugar and other West Indies products which were sold in ports throughout Europe. How much the American takeover of this trade cost France in lost freight charges and uncollected duties could only be estimated, but these estimates ranged from sizeable to enormous.[15] Worse, perhaps, French officials were forced to acknowledge that American provisioning, especially in wartime, had become vital to France's retention of these islands. The troops that retook Guadeloupe from the British in 1794 and the other French fighting in Saint Domingue depended as much on American foodstuffs (for which they often failed to pay) as did the island's civilian population.[16] Even in its fury against the Jay treaty, the French Directory flinched at the prospect of closing that traffic. If it were shut down, warned Foreign Minister Charles Delacroix, it would "deprive us of a resource which the misfortunes of war have too long rendered necessary to us.[17]

Third, besides losing much of her Indies trade, France also suffered from acutely unfavorable balances in her direct trade. Unable to sell Americans enough wine and brandy to pay for her imports of grain, salt meat, and tobacco, France made up her yearly deficits with cash. Painful enough in peacetime, this outflow of specie was excruciating in wartime for this cash flow benefitted London. The reason was that economically, the Americans were in the same position with England that the France was with America, they purchased more goods than they exported and they made up

---

15 Joseph Philippe Letombe, the French Consul General estimated that the French losses from tax evasion at 73 million livres, profits to slave importers at 22 million, and cargoes lost to French carriers at 371 million, Joseph Philippe Letombe, "Memoir," December 15, 1795

16 Ibid. Letombe found the Antilles trade "completely abandoned" to American merchants since 1793.

17 "Memoir to serve in developing part of the instructions of General Perignon relative to the retrocession of Louisiana," March 16, 1796, Acts du Directoire, I, 826

their deficit the same way as the French, with cash, French cash. France looked upon this circular flow of specie as tantamount to a French subsidy of the British war effort, with Americans as guilty intermediaries. An eyewitness to this process, former Vice-Consul of the Republic of France summed up the official sense of outrage. Asking rhetorically whether Americans had been willing to accept French imports, his angry retort was, "no, they have themselves paid off in good specie which has fed the manufactures of our cruelest enemy, England!"[18]

Behind this anger lay the reality that French exports had only a limited market in the United States. Although Americans consumed French wines and brandies, these items combined with French silks, laces, artificial flowers, and filigree in which French craftsmen specialized, never came close to equaling French purchases of foodstuffs and tobacco. Hopeful of altering this reality, the French government compiled an impressed file of proposed "solutions" which if they offered no easy answers, at least showed a widespread awareness of the problem. Duplaine, for example, urged the government to conduct a survey of the American market and then underwrite the manufacture of products found best suited to American tastes.[19] Similarly, the American merchant James Swan who, acting as a purchasing agent for the French navy also stressed the importance of tailoring French products to the American consumer.[20] In Philadelphia, Consul General Letombe saw a major handicap to French commerce in the haphazard timing of ship arrivals. French merchantmen, he noted, often arrived "out of season" weeks or even months after British cargoes had been landed

---

18 Peter P. Hill, Prologue to the Quasi-War: Stresses in Franco-American Commercial Relations, 1793-96, The *Journal of Modern History*, Vol. 49, No.1,(March, 1977), p D1046-D1047

19 A. C. Duplaine, "Notes," p. 200

20 "Plan of Commerce, No. 1, to both the Committees of Public Safety and of Finances, Paris, December 12, 1793, from Citizen Swan," f11 (Subsistances), carton 223, Archives Nationales de France.

and sold.[21] Joseph Fauchet, Minister Plenipotentiary of the French Republic to the United States saw a partial solution in a mutual lowering of duties and a lessening of trade restrictions. The American merchant community looking to increase their business urged the French to release American ships detained in the port of Bordeaux. Such a release would allow their cargoes to be sold which would help France meet her payments to the United States.[22]

The remedy to the commercial problems between the United States and France most sought by the French was a new treaty of commerce, which the French government believed would right the balance of payments. Joseph Fauchet explained to the Directory in early 1796 why he and his predecessors had failed: their powers had been inadequate, their instructions too vague, or they had met with American indifference.[23] While the Directory did seek a treaty solution, would it have been of any use? Even if the duties were lowered or the cargo restrictions eased, could that have possibly reversed the huge trade imbalance? And could such a treaty be negotiated in the face of American disinterest? And all of this occurred during a growing animus toward Jay's treaty which made any successful treaty negotiation unlikely. Looking at the entire situation, France's unfavorable balance of trade remained a problem without a viable solution and must looked at as the equal of Jays treaty as problems that France had with the United States.

Along with the commercial situation between the United States and France, was the commercial situation between the United States and England. In mid-1796, after the Jay treaty and before France took the harder line that would lead ultimately to the Quasi War, Delacroix listed the major causes that the French had with the

---

21 Ibid. p. 207, also the English merchants could cross the Atlantic unmolested, not so the French, it is difficult to keep a schedule when you are under fire.

22 This detention came as a result of an embargo laid on American ships by the city of Bordeaux from August 12, 1793 until the end of March 1794. The embargo was lifted following protests from Gouverneur Morris, the United States Minister at Paris and James Fenwick, the United States consul at Bordeaux.

23 Joseph Fauchet, "Memoir on the United States of America," March 20, 1796

return of relations between the United States and England. The first charge was that British warships were operating out of American ports to attack French shipping. Next was that Jays treaty classified naval stores (and perhaps also foodstuffs) as contraband. Finally that France's importation of these items now stood in jeopardy because no longer would neutral flag carriers be safe from British seizure.[24] Delacroix voiced these complaints to James Monroe, who wrote to Thomas Pickering, "France had much cause of complaint against us, independently of our treaty with England."[25] There are various reasons for Delacroix to have said this: frustrations with wartime commerce, or the daily encounters between American merchants and French officialdom which, in three years' time had so thoroughly exasperated the French establishment.

Twenty-five years earlier, France and the United States had met in a common enterprise which was mutually beneficial, now in the 1790's, they were together again, however this time the commonality was grievances. For example, while France visited some highly visible disruptions on American shipping, the self-punishing backlash she suffered in consequence has received less notice.

As to the first, by 1796 France had devised a myriad of Port controls under which American ships were delayed, often detained for long periods, and sometimes confiscated. Cargoes were restricted as to what goods could be bought, sold, landed, or laded. Crewmen and passengers were jailed if thought to be British subjects, or sometimes held merely on suspicion.[26] With a revolutionary zeal aimed at

---

24 Neither Article 12 nor 18 of Jay's treaty made clear the contraband status of provisions. Delacroix also complained of: U.S. judicial interference in French prize cases; the failure of the American Congress to empower French consuls to settle disputes among French citizens; and Fauchet's near capture by a British warship in U.S. waters. Albert H. Bowman, *The Struggle for Neutrality: Franco-American Diplomacy During the Federalist* Era (Knoxville, University of Tennessee Press, 1974), p. 246

25 Monroe to (Secretary of State) Pickering, Paris, February 20, 1796

26 Monroe to Edmund Randolph (Secretary of State before Pickering), Paris, September 15, 1794

marshaling the nation's resources, French officials saw themselves imposing on American shipping controls best suited to serve the cause of the Republic at war. By the use of these controls, the French government had three main objectives: to prevent imported goods (mainly from the United States) from being sold above what it considered "maximum" price levels, to keep French products of "first necessity", from being exported, and to prevent commerce that might aid Britain.

Price fixing and the prohibition of some exports began in September, 1793, when the French government tried to solve the twin problems of shortages and inflation. At the time some 40 commodities, mostly foodstuffs, textiles, and minerals were fixed in price and barred from export. Of the two restrictive categories, price fixing proved to be the most ephemeral. The Committee of Public Safety soon realized how ruinously France's import trade would suffer if neutral importers had to choose between selling cargoes at priced fixed loses or having their vessels detained for refusal to sell. On November 7, the French government retreated, announcing that items deemed "merchandise of the first necessity" might be sold to government agents at prices agreeable to both parties.

A greater problem that nations trading with the French faced was that when the government reduced exports to those goods not classified as "first necessity," it reduced the volume as well as the variety of outgoing cargoes, which further worsened the balance of payments, requiring a greater cash outlay, and additionally created widespread delays and ill will with its' trading partners.

By 1794, the trading situation between France and the United States had reached the point where it could have ceased altogether. In the same year, James Monroe arrived in Paris as American minister. After listening to the outraged shipmasters, he brought their grievances the Committee of Public Safety. France, he told them was accepting cargoes without paying for them, seizing others because they were enemy owned, delaying the departure of American ships,[27] and detaining individual persons without just cause.[28] Monroe then warned the Committee that such controls would soon cost France her neutral traffic, because merchants, already alarmed by news of French interference, would not long continue to send ships and cargoes to French ports.[29]

This warning from Monroe coupled with other reports from Frenchmen in the United States that American merchants were holding back shipments to France, caused alarm in the French capital.[30] Why these reports and the fact that the British were continuing to harass ocean shipments to France did not convince the French to relax their port controls suggests that Paris believed that it had no choice but to keep its control system intact to relieve, as much as possible its domestic shortages.

The French once again looked for a solution that would keep neutral shipping alive, but under French control. The first idea was to increase the number of neutral flag vessels that could ship product to France by selling French captured prize ships to neutral buyers. The idea originated with Jean Delbarade, the French Navy Commissioner, who realizing the problems of dealing with American carriers, urged his government to buy about 100 vessels from French prize masters, put them under neutral flags and send them out to carry French cargoes exclusively. If government ownership of the vessels proved to be too transparent, neutral merchants might be invited to "buy" these ships but in fact operate them under government contract. The Committee of Public Safety opted to institute a variation of Delbarade's plan. On November 14, 1794, the Committee authorized the sale of prize ships to neutral persons. In practice however, while

---

27 Those detained at Bordeaux as an example.

28   Gouverneur Morris to Edmund Randolph, September 15, 1794

29 Ibid.

30 Report from French Consul at Philadelphia, Jean Baptiste Petry to the Commission des Relations Exterieures told of widespread fears among American shippers.

some ships were sold, others were merely consigned. If sold, the buyer was required to use the vessel to serve French commercial interests. In either case, the two outcomes worked to the benefit of France. If the ship was stopped by the British, it would simply be another neutral vessel. Moreover, the number of relatively secure neutral carriers would be increased and would transport specified cargoes at those freight rates that would best supply France on her own terms.[31]

Historians have not been able to determine how many vessels would eventually be part of the program, however by October, 1795 the Navy Commission reported that that some of the purchases had been underwritten by commercial companies of dubious solvency and that these purchasers were leaving France with these vessels and not returning. Additionally, these "buyers" were suspected of having requested a neutral government to certify either the loss or unseaworthiness of these ships which allowed them to acquire bonafide neutral registry and thus escape French jurisdiction altogether. Although the Navy Commission did not specify Americans as the chief offenders, the context of their report left little doubt that they believed this to be the case.[32] The other idea to keep shipping under French control was to enlist Monroe's cooperation in modifying the port control situation to France's benefit. The reasoning here was that Monroe was thought be a likely abettor of any maritime policies that were fairly implemented. Also that Monroe in his official capacity, might have been able to win a measure of compliance from his fellow countrymen allowing France to administer her control system in ways less threatening to neutral traffic,[33] and finally Monroe, as a friend of revolutionary France, would do whatever he could to aid that nation. Neither idea was not only not successful in solving the problem, but only added to the French distrust of neutrals, especially Americans.

---

31 When the program failed to produce an adequate amount of cargo for France, the Navy Commission proposed giving subsidies to purchasers, however, this idea also failed to produce the needed ship borne supplies.

32 Navy Commission report mentioned by Commission de la Marine et des Colonies to Comite de Salut public, October 9, 1795

33 In fact, Monroe urged the committee to lift its controls entirely.

On May 9, 1793, the National Convention of France issued a
decree authorizing the seizure, on board a neutral vessel, of enemies'
goods or of provisions bound to an enemy's port, the latter to be paid
for and the vessel released upon the discharge of the cargo:

> Art. 1. Ships of war and privateers may seize and carry into
> the ports of the Republick, neutral vessels which are wholly or
> in part loaded with provisions, being neutral property bound to
> an enemy's port, or with merchandise belonging to an enemy.

> Art. 2. Merchandise belonging to an enemy is declared
> a lawful prize, seizable for the profit of the captor. Provisions
> being neutral property, shall be paid for at the price they would
> have sold for at the port where they were bound

> Art. 3. In all cases neutral vessels shall be released as soon as
> the unlading of the provisions or the seizure of the merchandise
> shall be effected. The freight shall settled at the rate paid by
> the charterers. A proper compensation shall be granted for the
> detention of the vessels by the tribunals, who are ready to judge
> the prizes.[34]

With this decree, the French government began to take actions
which would bring France into conflict with the United States,
although not continuously. The United States minister, Gouverneur
Morris, complained that this decree violated the twenty-third article
of the treaty of commerce of 1778, referring to the "free ships made
free goods" verbiage. The French immediately issued another decree
on May 23, assuring Morris that he would "find a new confirmation
of the principles from which the French people will never depart with
regard to their good friends and allies the United States of America."
Yet on the 28th of May, when a French privateer captured a rich
American ship, the decree of the 23rd was repealed. Upon continued
complaints from Morris, on July 1, another decree was issued
declaring "that the vessels of the United States are not compromised
in the regulations of the decree of the 9th of May"; but this was once

---

34   Gardner Weld Allen, *Our Naval War With France*, Appendix III, p. 298

more reversed on July 27, when the French declared that the decree of May 9th was in full force. For a year and a half this state of affairs continued with the confiscation of American vessels until the decree of May 9th, 1793 was finally repealed on January 3, 1795.

Another problem involving shipping was one of mistaken identity. Too often American seamen were treated harshly by the French because they were mistaken for Englishmen, and the French openly admitted that they could not tell the difference. As early as October, 1793, French Foreign Minister Francois Deforgues told Morris that "the difficulty of distinguishing our allies from our enemies has often been the cause of offence on board your vessels. . . ."[35] This uncertainty of nation "recognition" so often overlooked helps to explain the French preoccupation with passports, bills of lading, crew rosters, and other ships' papers, as well as delays embargoes, and imprisonments which ensued when these papers were not found in order. At dockside, it was almost certain that French port officials could not be sure that persons, ships, and cargoes claiming to be American were not in fact British. Additionally, laxities in American naturalization procedures made it easy for "enemy" Britons to acquire certification as "friendly" Americans. Also, when the British encountered a problem in acquiring American naturalization papers, they could simply resort to forgeries of American papers.

Monroe, attempting to solve this problem, noted that the confusion often began at sea when French naval officers became "embarrassed" because they could not tell the difference between American and British sailors, resulting in the "safe "assumption that they were dealing with a British seaman, and acted accordingly. Every French warship, he suggested should enlist one or two Americans as marine guards. These marines could easily tell the difference between British and American crews, and an added benefit, as Monroe saw it, the marines' close association with French officers would help strengthen the ties between the two countries. The Americans could

---

35 American State Papers, Foreign Relations, Paris, October 14, 1793, p.313

also gain experience in naval strategy from the French.[36] The last point evoked a negative response from Dalbarade. Asked for his opinion, the Navy Commissioner warned that "the only and real effect" of accepting Monroe's proposal would be "to make naval officers for the Americans in the school of the French navy." Was it prudent, he asked, "to expand the hope and the means which they already have . . . .?[37]

The French government did not give up attempting to elicit suggestions from Monroe to solve this problem, but the American Minister could see no way to prevent British shipmasters from forging American papers, although he admitted that U.S. consuls had made matters worse by issuing passports to Britons claiming to be Americans by way of naturalization.[38] Hoping to clarify the situation, the French on July 11, 1795 forbade resident ministers to issue passports except to fellow citizens who were native born, despite the blow to legally naturalized Americans. Monroe attempted to go both ways on this issue, he assured Philadelphia that he could still issue some "protections" while at the same time promising Paris that they would not be issued by U.S. consuls.

Even if the passport controversy had been solved, illicit trade would have continued virtually untouched. Although trade with Britain had been proscribed since October 9, 1793 by the French, American shipmasters showed remarkable skills in evading this proscription, so that by the middle of 1795, these breaches had constituted a major French grievance. In August, as an example, French officials in the port of Bordeaux reported that 30 to 40 ships flying the American flag were obviously running supplies to the British fleet blocking entrance to the port.[39] In the English Channel offenses were so frequent as to be termed "daily." Monroe was told by

---

36 Monroe to Comite de Salut public, November 29, 1794

37 Dalbarade to the Comite de Salut public, December 7, 1794

38 Monroe to Pickering, July 6, 1796

39 Administrators of the Marennes District to the Committee of General Safety, August 15, 1795

the French that these vessels flying the American flag were returning to the British fleets off the French coast at such short intervals that their cargoes could only been of British origin. The officials also told Monroe that these ships were also landing suspicious passengers, mail, and even specie.[40] When the French occupied the Netherlands, they found more problems with the current system. Here, American shipmasters, after certifying for French or neutral port destinations were actually selling their cargoes to the British. Even bonding requirements did not guarantee that American ships would not arrive at British ports. When they did dock at British ports, some captains claimed to have been "seized" and then demanded a refund of the bond on the grounds that they were forcibly diverted from their announced destinations.[41] Occasionally, American ships were detected in illicit trade, but for the most part French port officials had to be content to detain on suspicion or to simply allow neutral vessels to leave French ports without inspection.[42]

An American entrepreneur, James Swan, explained to the Committee of Public Safety just how easy it was for a neutral shipper to carry goods to France. Assuming, he stated, that you had a cargo designated for France shipped from either Europe or the United States. The basic safeguard, he explained was to carry the goods under a neutral flag. A cargo from Britain, for example, might be routed to Hamburg where it would be ostensibly redirected to Lisbon, but actually put in at the French port of Le Havre. Swan boasted to the Committee that he has actually used this method to bring a shipload of iron to France. Another way, when a bond was posted, and the cargo was coming from England was to station a French ship in the English Channel, which would go through the motions of "capturing" the cargo ship, and then take it into a French port.

---

40 Commission de la Marine et des Colonies to Monroe, August 15, 1795

41 Commission des Relations Exterieures to Comite de Salute public, October 16, 1795

42 One such departing vessel was overtaken and captured after its French pilot overheard that its destination was the British port of Guernsey. Commission de la Marine et des Colonies to Comite de Salut public, May 31, 1795

An even simpler way to accomplish the same objective was to raise a distress signal and then sail into a French port. The ship's captain would then plead either capture or distress and then recover his bond, meanwhile France would have the cargo that was ordered. The lesson should have been unmistakable: what Swan could accomplish as a purchasing agent for the French government, others could do to defeat the best laid plans for preventing traffic with Britain.[43]

The French also had problems due to their method of purchasing supplies in the United States. The French diplomat Edmond Genet had his agents make purchases unobtrusively and with a coordinated effort, so that as an example, these supply buys had little effect on American commodity prices in the year 1793. By 1794 however when Genet had lost his position with the French government and when more supplies were needed to fight the British, prices rose sharply because the purchasing became too widely publicized and because the number of French purchasing agents had multiplied. In the spring of 1794, Michel O'Mealy, a Baltimore commodity merchant, then living in Paris wrote to the French Supply Commission stating that its agents could expect to pay 25-33% above current prices if they came openly and in large numbers. O'Mealy urged that only one agent be sent and that he move quietly through the American port cities placing orders "for everything he wants before loading a single boat."[44] Instead four French agencies opening bought supplies that spring. They not only competed with one another, but also with British buyers, thereby raising prices. Worse still, in some cases they had to buy from speculators who had cornered the market for some needed merchandise. The French supply agents even lost the ability to buy on credit when the news broke that Admiral Pierre Jean Van Stabel's squadron was on the way to the United States carrying five

---

43 Swan was an extremely interesting individual, born in Scotland, he fought on the American side in the Revolutionary War. In the late 1780s, debt laden, he travelled to Paris joining a company that furnished supplies for the French government. In 1808, he was committed to a luxury prison for debt in which he remained until his death in 1830.

44 "General Observations on the proposed plan by the Committee for the purchase of commodities," Archives Nationales de France, carton 223

million francs, which prompted many wholesalers to demand cash. Finally, officials in Paris began to repeatedly urge greater secrecy and coordination in their American purchasing, but the French revolutionary bureaucracy never solved their purchasing problems. After years of negotiating with British merchants, the Americans had learned the ins and outs of making a profit while doing business. The French, engaged in a war and controlled by a revolutionary government that had recently executed their hereditary rulers, did not have the capacity at this time to engage in trade on an equal basis. Nevertheless, even though they knew that they had the support of the Jeffersonians, the blame for their inability to conduct business to their benefit with the United States, had to be with the Americans.

By summer, 1796, France was ready to strike at the United States. Reprisals against American shipping were authorized by a degree dated July 2:

All neutral or allied powers shall, without delay, be notified that the flag of the French Republick will treat neutral vessels, as to confiscation, as to search or detention [visiteou prehension], in the same manner as they shall suffer the English to treat them[45]

Before the end of August, Pierre Adet was told to convey to Philadelphia France's outrage at the commercial situation, and then to announce suspension of his own diplomatic function.[46] Although the Quasi-War did not follow immediately or even inevitably, the ensuing depredations on American commerce, taken in context with Adet's efforts to affect the outcome of an American presidential election, escalated tensions to a more dangerous level.[47] While

45 Gardner Weld Allen, *Our Naval War With France* (Miami, HardPress Publishing, 1909), Appendix III, p. 298

46 By this decree France threatened to treat neutral ships in the same manner as they allowed themselves to be treated by Britain, This decree was so imprecise that the French now allowed the seizure of American vessels on almost any pretext. Additionally, the Directory recalled Adet as ambassador to the United States.

47 Adet had worked for Adams's defeat in the election of 1796

France's hard line policy towards the United States derived principally from rancor at Jay's treaty, there was no doubt that its commercial problems were of almost equal importance.

By 1796, another factor allowed France to lash out at the Jay treaty. At this time the French armies were performing so well on the Continent that while American grain supplies, though still useful, were no longer vital. Now British interdiction combined with French naval impotence had made America's supply role uncertain and by late 1796, virtually superfluous. However, nothing had changed in other areas: American merchants still controlled the Antilles trade; in direct trade with France, the United States continued to buy less than it purchased from the French; and because American trade was unfavorably balanced towards Britain, French payments for imports for imports appeared to benefit America's British creditors. As far as French rules and regulations were concerned, Americans had not followed French maritime procedures, and the French could not hope to wage economic warfare against its "cruelest enemy" when they could not block cross channel traffic and regulate imports and exports. Finally, with few places to buy supplies, the French had to endure American pricing, which at times was extraordinarily high. Because of this situation, Frances' efforts to solve these problems either bred new frustrations or deepened her awareness of impotence, which helps to explain the deterioration of Franco-American relations.

On March 2, 1797, possibly in reaction to Adam's defeat of their supporter Jefferson for the presidency, the French Directory commissioned its warships and privateers to seize U.S. flagged vessels lacking satisfactory inventory records or containing items that the French deemed contraband:

> Art. V. Agreeably to the 21st article of the treaty of London of the 19th of November, 1794, every individual known to be American, who holds a commission given by the enemies of France, as also every mariner of that nation making a part of the crew of private or publick ships [naviresouvaisseaux] of the

enemy, shall be from that act alone declared a pirate and treated as such, without allowing him in any case to show that he had been forced by violence, menaces or otherwise.

Art. VI. In conformity to the law of the 14th February, 1793, the regulations of the 21st October, 1744, and of the 26th July, 1778, as to the manner of proving the right of property in neutral ships and merchandise, shall be executed according to their form and tenor. In consequence every American vessel shall be a good prize which has not on board a list of the crew [role d'equipage] in proper form, such as is prescribed by the model annexed to the treaty of the 6th February, 1778, a compliance with which is ordered by the 25th and 27th articles of the same treaty.

These items violated American shipping rights under its 1778 treaty with France; further, it gave American ships no time to comply, making the entire U.S. merchant fleet fair game for French marauders.[48] The French confiscated one American merchant ship, the schooner *Industry* and its entire cargo simply because its *role d'equipage* (list of crew and passengers) had been "signed only by one notary public, without the confirmation of witnesses."[49]

In creating these proclamations, France did not seek to conquer the United States. Therefore the Directory publicly denied that France was at war, while it privately plotted to destabilize President Adams's administration. The minister of foreign relations, Charles Delacroix, maintained that France was at war with the federal government, but not with the American people[50] At a special session of Congress less than three months into his presidency, Adams warned of the Directory's "disposition to separate the people of the United States

48 Stanley Elkins and Eric McKitrick, *The Age of Federalism: The Early American Republic,* 1788-1800 (New York: Oxford University Press, 1993) p. 537

49 *Cushing v. United States,* 22 Ct. Cl. 1, 3-4 (1886)

50 Alexander DeConde, *The Quasi-War: The Politics and Diplomacy of the Undeclared War with France,* 1797-1801 (New York: Charles Scribner's Sons, 1966), p. 457

from the government."[51] The Directory hoped to inspire a popular revolution in America that would topple the Adams's administration, much as the French Revolution had deposed Louis XVI. To achieve this result without alienating the American people and driving the United States into a military alliance with Britain, France conducted a war of limited scale, forces, and military objectives.

The major financial French gain from the decrees of March, 1797 was plunder, which was encouraged by renting French warships to privateers and also taking payoffs from these privateers whose captures they upheld in admiralty courts. American seamen on captured U. S. vessels were either stranded or marched off to prison.[52] Those found on British ships faced worse treatment. The Directory announced that France would hang as pirates any Americans found serving on British warships, even those whom the British had pressed into service.[53]

After a Paris coup d'etat in September 1797 put hard-liners in control, the Directory issued the following decree on January 18, 1798:

Art. 1. The character of vessels in what concerns their quality as neutral or enemy shall be decided by their cargo; in consequence every vessel found at sea, laden in whole or in part with merchandise coming [provenants] from England or her possessions, shall be declared good prize, whoever may be the proprietor of these productions or merchandise.[54]

The decree was issued on the pretence of confiscating British contraband, but in reality the intent was to punish the American government for signing Jay's treaty. The decree came without warning, offered no prospect of reconciliation, and far exceeded in severity

---

51 Ibid. p. 18

52 John Adams's Message to the House of Representatives, February 15, 1799

53 Ibid.

54 Gardner Weld Allen, *Our Naval War With France*, Appendix III, p.299

the alleged transgressions.[55] This decree permitted confiscation of a U.S. ship having nothing more than a British-made compass on board. Since nearly every American ship contained some article of British manufacture, any ship stopped by a French privateer was almost certain to be taken as a prize. A French corsair confiscated the schooner *Little Pegg* solely because its captain was a naturalized U.S. citizen of Scottish birth.[56]

The Directory was content with this policy since it lost little by the existing situation, and it did not believe that the United States would declare war.[57] France planned to await overtures of conciliation from the American government. Letombe, the French consul general in Philadelphia who took over Adet's functions in May, 1797, assured Adams and Jefferson that France did not intend a rupture and that all could be put right if America would send a minister whose character guaranteed a change of attitude toward France.[58]

55 Abraham D. Sofaer, *War, Foreign Affairs, and Constitutional Power* (New York: Harper Collins, 1977), p. 139

56 *Cushing v. United States*, 1,8

57 Delacroix to Adet, April 1, 1797

58 Ibid.

John Adams

Pierre August Adet

Fisher Ames

Napolean Bonaparte

Steven Decatur

Oliver Ellsworth

Albert Gallatin

Elbridge Gerry

Citizen Genet formally
presented to Washington

Alexander Hamilton

Impressment of American Seaman [by British Navy]

John Jay

Thomas Jefferson

Rufus King

Marquis de Lafayette

James Madison

John Marshall

James Monroe

Gouverneur Morris

Horatio Nelson

Timothy Pickering

Charles Cotesworth Pinckney

Talleyrand

Chapter 5

American Preparedness For War

A t the time when Franco-American relations began to deteriorate, the United States had no armed naval vessels whatever. The last surviving war ship of the Revolutionary War, the frigate *Alliance* had been sold in 1785. Of the few officers and crews remaining, most were in the merchant marine.

No sooner had the old navy disappeared than the need for such a force began to be appreciated. In 1785, two American merchantmen were seized by Algerine pirates and their crews enslaved. Jefferson, then minister to France began at once to urge the necessity of a naval force to protect American commerce in the Mediterranean. A committee of Congress in 1786 and a Senate committee in 1791 reported favorably on the subject, but nothing came of it. It was not until the capture of eleven more vessels by the Algerines in 1793 that Congressional debate on the wisdom of reviving the navy began in earnest. In his annual address to Congress on December third, President Washington spoke in general terms of the nation's need to prepare to defend itself: "If we desire to avoid insult, we must be able to rebel it: if we desire to secure peace. . . ., it must be known, that we are at all times ready for War."[1] A few days later, news reached Philadelphia of the truce between Portugal and Algiers, opening the way for the Barbary corsairs to cruise the Atlantic and

---

1   George Washington, "Fifth Annual Address to Congress," 3 December, 1793

imperil trade with much of Europe.[2] On December 16, the President forwarded to Congress documents on the unsatisfactory negotiations with the Barbary Powers. In response to these events, the House of Representatives resolved on January 2, 1794 "that a naval force adequate to the protection of the commerce of the United States, against the Algerine corsairs, ought to be provided,"[3] and appointed a committee to prepare a report on what kind of naval force would be necessary to deal with the menace. On January 20, 1794, committee chairman Thomas Fitzsimons, a Federalist from Pennsylvania, reported a resolution to authorize the procurement of six frigates, a force thought sufficient for the purpose.

Despite the real threat to American commerce, congressional approval of naval legislation was far from certain. By the 1790s, there were differing opinions about the need for any increase in the nation's armed forces. Those opposed argued that navies posed a greater danger to liberty than did armies. They maintained that the major expense of constructing, fitting out, and manning warships meant large expenditures and mounting taxes, and they considered this transfer of wealth from the people via politicians into the hands of a few to be a source of political corruption. Influenced by these beliefs, several congressmen spoke in opposition to the proposal to procure the six frigates. Some surmised that the Algerines were acting on behalf of the British and that going to war with the former would risk a Anglo-American conflict. They further believed that paying a bribe to the Algerines would be wiser and cheaper than building a navy. One Congressman even suggested the alternative of hiring the Portuguese Navy to protect American commerce. Opponents of the naval measure also questioned whether the six frigates would be enough to protect American interests.

The pro navy side was strengthened when the President sent

---

2   Before the treaty with Algiers, Portugal blocked the Algerine warships from leaving the Mediterranean.

3   U. S. Congress, *American State Papers. Documents, Legislative and Executive, of the Congress of the United States*, 38 Vols. (Washington: Gales and Seaton, 1832-61), Class VI, Naval Affairs, 1:5

documentation supporting his view that a navy was essential and by the almost simultaneous news that the British had prohibited all neutral trade with the West Indies. The Act that passed the Congress provided for the six frigates, four of forty-four guns and two of thirty-six, passed the House by a vote of fifty to thirty-nine. The voting mainly regional, those voting in favor were from the state's most concerned with maritime trade – The north and east. Opponents came from rural areas - the south and the frontier. The act passed the Senate and became law on March 27, 1794.

Secretary of War, Henry Knox, responsible for the construction of the ships, reported to Congress in December, 1794 that passing the act:

> . . . .created an anxious solicitude that this second commencement of a navy for the United States should be worthy of their national character. That the vessels should combine such qualities of strength, durability, swiftness of sailing, and force, as to render them equal, if not superior, to any frigates belonging to any of the European Powers.[4]

His succinct phrase, "this second commencement of a navy for the United States," summarized the resounding significance of this act. The "anxious solicitude" felt by the nation's leaders led to the building of these warships. The next phase was the actual construction. Rather than purchasing merchant ships and converting them into men-of-war, an option under the act, Secretary Knox, head of the Department of War, recommended the construction of new frigates designed to be superior to any vessel of that class in the European navies. To keep labor costs down, Knox mandated that the ships would be constructed by government employees rather than private contractors. Politically, to spread out the economic benefits and to win popular support, he also distributed the construction sites geographically. "It is just and wise to proportion . . . .benefits as nearly as may be to those places or states which pay the greatest

---

4   Ibid., 6.

amount to its support, a few thousand dollars in expenses will be no object compared with the satisfaction a just distribution would afford."[5]

The warships were still being framed when, in early 1796, the United States entered into a negotiated peace with Algiers, at the cost of nearly one million dollars, which included a ransom payment for captured American prisoners and the cost of building the 32-gun frigate *Crescent* for the Dey's fleet. The act authorizing the six frigates had called for a halt in construction in the event of peace with Algiers, but President Washington urged Congress to extend authorization to complete the warships. Congress then approved the completion of three of the six frigates, allowing the remained to remain in their partially constructed state.

During 1797, the Congress again took up the issue of the warships, remaining divided over whether or not to complete them. In July however because of continuous French attacks on American commerce, Congress authorized the completion of the ships.

Early in the Quasi War with France, citizens in a number of American cities reacted differently from their Congress, deciding to retaliate. Since the United States had no warships, they began in late 1796 to initiate subscriptions for private funding to construct warships that would protect American property at sea. Their motivation was simultaneously patriotic and self-serving. Many of the subscribers were merchants, shippers, or ship owners whose incomes were being adversely affected by the French attacks.

A review of the situation reveals why these individuals decided to take action. From October 1796 to June 1797, the French captured 316 U. S. vessels - more than 6 percent of the nation's merchant ships - causing their owners losses of $12 million to $15 million. Newburyport, Massachusetts alone claimed to have lost 77 ships and their cargoes worth $682,000 from 1797 to 1799. Philadelphia merchants claimed to have lost $2 million because of the French actions. Moreover, during 1797, general marine insurance rates rose

---

5   Henry Knox to George Washington, April 15, 1794

on cargoes travelling to the West Indies alone to seven times their previous level. In the face of such conditions, fewer voyages were being attempted. One of the more damaging effects experienced during 1797 and 1798 was a reversal of the previously rapid growth in both imports and exports. This diminution of international trade affected all Americans, not only those in maritime industries.

In March 1798, Secretary of War, James McHenry brought before Congress the problem of his responsibility for naval affairs. Naval administration had become a significant portion of his department's work, as it had for the Department of the Treasury, which oversaw all the navy's contracting and disbursing. The Department of War also had received congressional criticism for what was seen as the mismanagement and the excessive cost of the naval construction program. In addition, the growing threat posed by the French induced Congress to authorize an increase in size of the navy and raised the possibility that the navy would be called upon to confront French warships.

In response to the obvious need for an executive department responsible solely for, and staffed with persons competent in naval affairs, Congress passed a bill establishing a Department of the Navy which was signed by President Adams on April 30, 1798. To provide protection from enemies such as the French was obviously the U.S. Navy's primary mission, but the navy at the time did not exist as a fighting force, having no operational warships.

On July 11, the Congress formally established the Marine Corps. In doing so, it institutionalized a practice begun during the Revolution. Since that time naval captains had tapped their toughest officers and crew to act as marines. In battle, these men would grab muskets, scramble up the riggings to precarious perches, and try to pick off enemy officers and gunners. When the ships ground against each other, they would leap on to the enemy vessel, yelling madly, using their cutlasses and pistols. Now, the marines would be organized into detachments, officered, trained, and allocated among the nation's warships.

The army received a boost on July 16, when Congress authorized its expansion from four to sixteen infantry regiments of seven hundred troops each, along with six troops of light dragoons of fifty troopers each.

The President and the Congress began in 1798 to support the effort to protect American commerce. On May 28, Congress authorized the public vessels of the United States to capture armed French ships hovering off the coast of the United States, which effectively initiated the undeclared Quasi War with France. Next came the rapid passage of several pieces of naval legislation. An act of June 30 gave the President authority to accept ships on loan from private citizens. On July 9, Congress authorized U.S. naval vessels to capture armed French vessels anywhere on the high seas, not just off the nation's coast. This act also sanctioned the issuance of commissions to privateers. Two days later the President signed the act that officially established the United States Marine Corps.

At this point in 1798, the navy had the original three frigates, the *United States*, the *Constellation*, the *Constitution,* and little else. The void was filled by private subscribers who sought to build the vessels so desperately needed. Some historians have suggested that these ships were merely lent to the navy, others contend that the ship, once completed, became government property. If the vessels were merely lent to the government, then those that survived would have been returned eventually to the local groups that financed their construction. Yet in a ship by ship history of this era, there is no evidence that any of the subscription ships were returned to their owners.[6]

Moreover, these projects seem to have been true private initiatives:

> The private American citizens who conceived of these ships, put up the money, arranged for the designs, selected

---

6   Donald L. Canny, *The Sailing Warships of the U.S. Navy* (Annapolis: Naval Institute Press, 2001), p. 50-57

the timber and materials, laid the keels and planked up the hulls, selected the officers, and sent the ships off to war. Into each ship they put their experience, belief in their country, and their confidence in the future. The subscription warships were a compelling expression that that society's projection of itself.[7]

Historians debate whether this outpouring of "civic spirit" in providing the subscription ships was spontaneous, or as a result of the Act of June 30, authorizing the government to accept armed vessels from its citizens, with 6 percent interest. It would seem from a perusal of the facts that the statute merely reflected what American citizens were doing on their own. In diverse parts of the United States thousands of dollars were being raised by citizens without government sanction or direction. The Senate bill did not pass before subscriptions in Newburyport [Massachusetts], Philadelphia and New York were well under way, and the Senate bill was not printed in newspapers until Baltimore had begun its list. The House did not take up the bill before Norfolk, Richmond, and Petersburg, Virginia, had also entered the subscription frenzy.

If the merchants in the various subscription cities had been driven primarily by purely monetary concerns, why would they go to all the trouble of building warships in exchange for a 6 percent return when they could, with less effort, simply invest their funds in alternative, ordinary ways and gain a much higher return? The explanation seems unavoidable: they were not simply seeking an easy means of making a profit by responding to an offer by the federal government. They were genuinely outraged by the French attacks on American vessels on the high seas, and they perceived the existing U.S. naval forces as inadequate to the task of defending U.S. commerce.

Not surprisingly, the cites involved were almost all seaports. Besides those mentioned earlier, they included Salem and Boston, Massachusetts; Providence, Rhode Island; Charlestown, South

7 Frederick C. Leiner, *Millions for Defense: The Subscription Warships of 1798* (Annapolis: Naval Institute Press, 2000), p. 2

Carolina; and Norwich, Connecticut. To gain an idea of the monetary value of these purchases, consumer prices are now (2017) approximately twelve times higher than in 1800. Therefore as examples, Bostonians contribution of $136,000 was equal to $1.63 million today, Baltimore's $100,00 to $1.2 million and Salem's $75,000 to $900,000.[8]

The other factor to consider was that these cities were at the end of the eighteen century basically large towns. If Boston's population of 24,937 were divided into its' money raised, the result would be an average of $15,879 per inhabitant. This in an era when a skilled ship carpenter earned a dollar and a half per day in wages and a common laborer, a dollar. In addition, not only did the subscribers commit themselves to bear significant costs, but once completed and handed over to the federal government to prosecute the Quasi War against the French navy and privateers, the benefits from a given city's ship would not accrue to that city alone, but to America generally. Americans voluntarily contributed warships were suggestive of a high degree of citizenship.

The privately funded frigates represented a 62.5 percent increase in the number of warships of the largest type the United States possessed. Of the nine privately funded warships, four were small to medium sized frigates, and four were sloops of war.[9] The question has been asked, why didn't the builders of subscription ships build larger vessels? One reason was although admittedly impressive, they were expense to build. Perhaps more important, the conflict with France may have called for a different naval response. Most of the U.S. naval losses were to French privateers that were typically fast, maneuverable, of modest size, and not heavily armed. The smaller American frigates and sloops possessed more than enough firepower and speed to defeat the French vessels. As secretary

---

8   *Ibid.* p.185

9   Frigates were the second largest war ships at this time. The largest were known as ships-of-the-line which carried 64-120 guns. The U.S. Navy possessed no ships-of-the-line until after the War of 1812. Frigates carried 24 to 60 guns and sloops of war 18-28 guns.

of the Navy Benjamin Stoddert stated, "[O]nly fast vessels could be effective against the French."[10] Moreover the hypothesis that nimble, speedy ships were crucial to success in the Quasi War with France is bolstered by the fact that all of the nine privately built ships seemed to have been designed to be uncommonly fast. A current naval historian concurs with this train of thought, "Given the character of the conflict at hand, it seems obvious that the smaller ships were of much more utility in dealing with the French privateers and in handling commerce protection tasks."[11]

The subscription vessels were mainly designed by or build under the direction of Joshua Humphreys, a Philadelphia shipbuilder who was not only looking for speed, but also the construction of warships that because of the small size of the American Navy would be superior to those warships of the European navies now and in the future:

> Ships that compose the European navys are generally distinguished by their rates;[12] but as the situation and depth of water of our coasts and harbors are different in some degrees from those in Europe, and as our navy for a considerable time will be inferior in numbers, we are to consider what size ships will be most formidable and be an overmatch for those of an enemy; such frigates as in blowing weather would be an overmatch for double-deck ships, and in light winds to evade coming to action; or double-deck ships that would be an overmatch for common double-deck ships, and in blowing weather superior to ships of three decks, or in calm weather or light winds to outsail them. Ships built on these principles will render those of an enemy in a degree useless, or require a greater number before they dare attack out ships. Frigates I suppose

---

10 Geoffrey M. Footner, *Tidewater Triumph: The Development and Worldwide Success of the Chesapeake Bay Pilot Schooner* (Centerville, Md. : Tidewater Publications, 1998), p. 84

11 Donald L. Canney, *The Sailing Warships of the U.S. Navy*, p. 116

12 A system of classifying ships, e.g. ship-of-the-line, frigate, sloop, etc.

will be the first object, and none ought to be built less than 150 feet keel, to carry twenty-eight 32 pounders[13] or thirty 24 pounders on the gun deck and 12 pounders on the quarter deck. . . .Frigates built to carry 12 and 18 pounders, in my opinion, will not answer the expectation contemplated from them, or if we should be obliged to take part in the present European war, or at a future day we should be dragged into a war with any powers of the Old Continent, especially Great Britain, they having such a number of ships of that size that it would be an equal chance by equal combat that we lose our ships.[14]

The first vessel of the navy to get to sea in the spring of 1798 was the warship *Ganges* carrying 24 guns, which sailed from Philadelphia on May 24. The *Ganges* was a vessel acquired by purchase, having been initially in service as a merchant ship. The ship was directed to cruise between Long Island and the Virginia capes for the protection of waters within the jurisdiction of the United States. The captains orders were limited, inasmuch as Congress had not authorized captures. The orders were changed on May 28 when American naval vessels were specifically "directed to seize, take, and bring into any port of the United States" any French armed vessel "which shall have committed, or which shall be found hovering on the coast of the United States for the purpose of committing, depredations on the vessels belonging to the citizens thereof."[15]

Earlier in May of the same year, President Adams and Secretary of War Thomas Pickering appointed Benjamin Stoddert, a prominent Maryland Federalist as Secretary of the Navy. Stoddard was actually a second choice, the first was George Cabot, another Federalist, who turned down the position, believing that he lacked the strength to be successful in the post. Although a second choice, he was a veteran

---

13 Cannon

14 Gardner Weld Allen, *Our Naval War With France* (Miami, HardPress Publishing, 1909), p. 41

15 Naval Chronicles, p. 90-92; Naval Correspondence in War, Department 304, Stoddert to Dale

of the Continental Army during the Revolution having served as secretary of the Continental Congress's Board of War. Harold and Margaret Sprout in *The Rise of American Naval Power, 1776-1918*, considered Stoddert one of the few Americans with "a clear grasp of the naturally strong strategic position of the United States, and at least a partial knowledge of the function and utility of capital ships in a system calculated to make the most of our geographic isolation."[16]

The effort expanded patrolling the coast during 1798 was worthwhile, even though few French ships were captured off the American shore because simple possession of a naval force served to scare away most French privateers. Also, the activity was useful for the ships and men of the navy. As warships were outfitted and sent to sea, usually for the first time, they patrolled off a friendly coast close to their home ports. Officers and men had time to work out the daily routines of naval life on board strange new ships. Captains exercised their crews, many of whom, even if good seamen (which most were not), were without military experience. All of this was accomplished in an atmosphere where little threat of combat existed. Even the limited experience gained in these early patrols was worth the effort, especially the establishment of routines for convoying.

In addition to the new warships that were built and the subscription vessels, the navy also relied heavily on converted ships. These transmuted trading vessels varied greatly in size, performance, and quality. The two main reasons were; first in a haste to buy a stopgap navy, the government paid for ships ill suited for conversion, and secondly many captains eager for glory in action with the French remodeled their ships (e.g. adding too many guns) to the point that the vessel's sailing qualities was ruined.

On July 7, 1798, the American naval warship *Delaware* under the command of Steven Decatur, Sr. encountered the French schooner *la Croyable* outside Egg Harbor, New Jersey. The French captain assumed the *Delaware* to be English since their belief was that the

16 Harold and Margaret Sprout, *The Rise of American Naval Power, 1776-1918*
   (Princeton: Princeton University Press, 1939), p. 42-43

United States had no navy, a belief shared by most vanquished French commanders during the Quasi War. The master of the la Croyable after the capture of his ship by Decatur complained that France and the United States were not at war, Decatur reminded his prisoner that the French had been making war on America for some time and now the Yankees would take care of themselves. Embarrassed by his capture, the French captain told Decatur that he would have gone down fighting had he known the Delaware to have been American. Decatur replied that he would "have been gratified if he had stood on board his vessel and fought her."[17]

Now that American warships were beginning to venture out to take on the French, the War Department had to deal with the problem of supplying the ships with military supplies. With the new naval construction planned, American military manufacturers were unable to produce sufficient quantities of acceptable ordinance. The main problem initially was cannons, while there was enough to outfit the few ships ready to sail in 1798, there was no effective management of the available resources, forcing captains to forage for armament.

On assuming responsibility for the nation's naval affairs, Stoddert found that cannon were but one of several items in short supply. The ships also needed; copper, canvas, hemp, gunpowder, muskets, and edged weapons. Importation, particularly from Great Britain substantially supplemented domestic production since American foundries failed to meet the government's expectations. It would not be until 1800 that Stoddert felt confident enough to report to Congress that "The manufacture of cannon, and indeed all kinds of arms, and military stores, is now so well established in the United States, that no want of them can be experienced in future, nor does it appear essential that large supplies of them should be laid up in store for the navy."[18]

17 United States Navy Department, Office of Naval Records and Library, Naval Documents Related to the Quasi- War with France: Naval Operations, February 1797-December 1801, Dudley W. Knox, ed., 7 vols.(Washington, D.C., 1935-1938), 1: p. 175-176

18 *Ibid*. V: p. 58

In July 1798, Stoddert began operations in the Caribbean to let the French know that the United States possessed both the will and the ability to engage the French privateers in that area. Stoddert's sources of intelligence, essentially whatever information reached the Navy Department from insurers, merchants, seamen, and the British, indicated that the French naval forces in the Caribbean were weak. The task was given to John Barry. [19]In a letter to Barry giving him this command, Stoddert wrote, "a small squadron, under the command of an officer of your intelligence, experience & bravery might render essential service, & animate your country to enterprise, by picking up a number of prizes in the short cruise to the islands."[20]

While Barry's instructions were fairly detailed, Stoddert was wise enough to realize that he could not direct operations within the Caribbean from Philadelphia. Barry was given the authority to act as he saw fit, in keeping with the main goals of the operation:

The object of the enterprise is, to do as much injury to the armed vessels . . . .of France & to make as many captures as possible, consistently with a due regard (& more than a due regard you will not suffer to be paid) to the security of our own-and you will use your best means to accomplish this object." Barry was free to depart from his instructions, if "expedient or necessary." Even the two months' time allotted the cruise was not rigid. Stoddert wrote that the length of the operation would "depend upon such a variety of circumstances that no accurate judgment can be formed of the time of your return."[21]

---

19 John Barry, generally credited with being the Father of the U.S. Navy. He fought with great distinction during the Revolutionary War and in 1794, he became the new U.S. Navy's first commissioned officer. During the Quasi War, captaining his flagship, the *United States*, Barry captured a number of French ships and also used his ship as a hands-on training facility.

20 Michael A. Palmer, *Stoddert's War: Naval Operations During the Quasi War with France,* 1798-1801 (Columbia, South Carolina: University of South Carolina Press, 1987), p. 36

21 William Bell Clark, *Gallant John Barry,* 1745-1803: *The Story of a Naval Hero of Two Wars* (New York: Macmillan Company, 1938), p. 203-204

On July 21, Barry captured his first prize of the war, the *Sans Peril* 10.[22] Other than that, the cruise was uneventful, and he returned the capital on September 21. In his report, he stated that he returned because his stores were rotting and because the hurricane season was approaching. As far as Stoddert was concerned however, the cruise was a disappointment, because Barry failed to follow the bulk of his instructions - not delivering letters, dividing his force, but mainly for not ignoring the hurricanes and staying on station.

Stoddert viewed the protection of American commerce as the immediate task of the navy. The greatest threat to trade lay in the Caribbean, posing special problems since American merchant ships sail to the area year round, their protection was a continuous requirement for the American navy.

On October 16, an incident occurred that outraged the administration. Captain Isaac Philips in command of a nine ship convoy came upon a British fleet under the command of Commodore John Loring. A British officer came aboard Philip's ship while Philips was not aboard. When Philips returned the officer claimed that many the American ship's crew were "Englishmen" and impressed them. While of the fifty-five American crewmen were taken off the American, fifty were returned later in the day, the damage was done.

President Adams upon hearing of the incident issued the following order:

> It is the positive command of the president, that on no pretence whatever you permit the public vessel of war under your command, to be detained, or searched, nor any of the officers or men belonging to her, to be taken from her, by the ships or vessels of any foreign nation, so long as you are in a capacity to repel such outrage on the honor of the American flag;-if force should be exerted to compel your submission, you are to resist that force to the utmost of you power-and when

---

22 The number after the name of the ship indicates the number of cannons on board.

overpowered by superior force, you are to strike your flag and thus yield your vessel as well as your men-but never your men without your vessel. . . .[23]

The message was clear to America's naval captains. Their duty was to defend their vessels and American honor against all odds. The first test of that policy occurred in March 1799 when the British frigate, *Surprise*, stopped the American brig *Ganges*, and its captain demanded that all British sailors be surrendered. Although he was outgunned two to one, the American captain, Thomas Tingey, issued a defiant written reply in capital letters: "A public ship carries no protection but her flag. I do not expect to succeed in a contest with you, but I will die at my quarters before a man will be taken from this ship."[24] The British ship promptly sailed away. Tingey has courageously scored a triumphant victory against the Royal Navy without a shot being fired.

As far as Phillips was concerned, he was dismissed from the Navy, the reasons given - Halting his convoy because of a command from a British captain, and secondly, following the orders of a British lieutenant.

At the end of 1798, Stoddert began to plan his winter offensive, taking into consideration Great Britain's policy towards the United States and her naval dispositions in American waters. The Americans were, after all, latecomers to a European conflict already in its seventh year. While the same French warships that attacked Yankee traders also attacked British merchantmen, there was no alliance between the two nations against the French. Both nations attempted an alliance in June 1798, but the price was too high for the Americans to participate - in exchange for the loan of warships, and British officers serving in the U.S. Navy at half pay, the British wanted to recruit American seamen for service in the Royal Navy. There was however some cooperation, first in the use of mutual recognition

23 United States Navy Department, Office of Naval Records and Library, p. 26-27

24 Alexander DeConde, The Quasi-War, p. 203

signals to be used at sea and the joining of American merchantmen in convoys escorted by British warships.

In planning the offensive, Stoddert also had to take into consideration the supplies need to keep the ships operational away from port. The goods consumed by the infant American navy were by modern standards, insignificant. At its peak strength during the Quasi War, the navy contained fewer than 6,000 men. Today a full compliment for a single *Nimitz*-class carrier is 6,286 officers and men. To provide for its personnel during the war, the Navy Department had to procure about 5,000 tons of provisions each year, with about half of that amount supplied to the ships on station in the Caribbean.

To solve the problem, Stoddert set up a small three ship squadron in the Caribbean, then in January 1799 chartered a merchant ship loaded with supplies to the squadron which would then be dispersed among the stationed ships. The logistical system developed during the winter of 1798-99 enabled Stoddert to maintain significant forces in the West Indies throughout the Quasi War.

During February 1799, another incident involving the British occurred, this time the American captain was Stephen Decatur Sr. whose convoy was approached by the British warship *Solebay*. The British captain had orders to search for contraband on all vessels bound for Havana. Decatur went alongside the British frigate, whose captain informed him of his desire to search the American ships. Decatur replied that he was of equal force and the there would be no search, and then simply sailed away. Upon his return to Philadelphia in May, Decatur received only praise for his actions and was promoted to the command of the frigate of his choice.

An instance of the French attempting to avoid the loss of a warship after a battle occurred on February 9, 1799. Thomas Truxtun captain of the *Constellation*, sailing south of Bermuda came upon the French warship *l'Insurgente* 36 and gave chase. The chase and the ensuing battle lasted for over four hours until the Frenchman surrendered. When Captain Barreaut of the *l'Insurgente* boarded the Constellation, he asked Truxtun, "Why have you fired on our national flag? Our two nations are not at war. Truxtun replied with his own question, "Your name sir, and that of your ship?"

"I am Capitaine de Fregate-Citizen Michel-Pierre Barreaut, commanding the French national frigate l'Insurgente of forty guns." "You, sir are my prisoner."

The next day, Barreaut repeated his surprise and indignation at being taken by an American ship.

"Why was our national flag fired upon? I am surprised that America has declared war."

Truxtun must have been puzzled: "America has not declared war against France!"

"Pardon me," Barreaut replied, "your taking me with a ship of the French nation is a declaration of war."

"If a capture of a national vessel is a declaration of war," retorted Truxtun, "your taking the *Retaliation*[25] commanded by lieutenant Bainbridge, which belonged to the United States and regularly placed in our navy, was certainly a declaration of war on the part of France against the United States.

To this Barreaut apparently had no response. Truxtun continued.

"Whether be it war or be it peace, I will certainly take every French frigate that I meet, and other French armed vessels as well, and you can tell that to General Desfourneaux.[26]"

---

25 Barreaut had shared in the capture of the *Retaliation* only two and a half months before and knew from that incident that the Americans, despite their lack of a declaration of war, had authorized their warships to take any French armed ship, public or private on the high seas.

26 Governor of Guadeloupe

The conversation ended.[27]

During December 1798 and January 1799, every ship in the American navy, save one, received orders for the Caribbean. In the spring of 1799, Stoddert looked toward a better performance of the navy with the combination of the war ships already in operation with new ships preparing for sea. Stoddert's plans however began to go awry, fifteen of the twenty ships on station in the Caribbean began to return to American ports during this time, for resupply.

Stoddert was both disappointed and embarrassed. Over a dozen American naval vessels were in port at the same time-competing with one another and the new ships, for men, naval stores, and provisions. Adams was aware of what had occurred; to the president the problem was clear and the solution simple. "There are too many ships in our ports. . . .every exertion ought to be made to get them to sea as soon as possible.." Stoddert too was disappointed.[28]Responsibility for the fiasco rested with the secretary of the navy, and his orders of December 1798 ambiguously gave the period April-June as the end of the operation.

The next situation that Stoddert became involved in was political. As the navy grew, so did the demands made of it. Federalist congressmen, reflecting the desires of their constituents, made increasing numbers of requests for a naval presence worldwide. To this point the navy's convoying duties had been limited to the Caribbean where Stoddert believed the navy's more important objectives lay:

Our first care ought to be, the security of our own coast-the next to avail ourselves of the commercial and perhaps political advantages which the present state of the West Indies & Spanish America, is calculated to afford us. By attending to these objects it may be possible to produce such strong conviction of dependence

---

27 The Truxtun-Barreaut conversations are drawn from their official reports, the indirect being converted into direct discourse.

28 United States Navy Department, Office of Naval Records and Library, p. 272-273

on the United States, that it may be difficult thereafter to arm these countries against us. It would be a great point gained in a war with France, that they should be obliged to make their attacks from Europe. At any rate, it seems to be in the power of France to shut us out from almost the whole of Europe-and perhaps our only means of compensation are to be found nearer home.[29]

Nevertheless, Stoddert was eager to do something for the merchants whose political support the navy needed. He was also not adverse to making a show of force in European waters. In the end, these latter considerations overcame his strategic good sense, however by the time he finalized his planning, the season had grown too late for the European operation.

From the beginning of his tenure as secretary, Stoddert had believed that quality officers were of greater importance to the service than mighty men-of-war. The way he put it, Unless commanders with "zeal & spirit" were found to command its ships, the United States "had better burn its vessels.[30]By the summer of 1799, few of Stoddert's captains had gained his approval. Of the six senior officers, only Truxtun had demonstrated possession of the of the requisite traits of command, as he saw it. Even John Barry, the navy's first ranked captain showed little interest in sailing "in harm's way."

After a year as secretary, Stoddert was wholly dissatisfied with his corps of officers. Their quality as seamen and commanders was uneven. Many were triflers. They were concerned too much with rank and prestige at the expense of the interests of the navy. When they failed to have their way, they transferred to the merchant service, where they began. Stoddert was not about to "burn" his ships in response to this situation, but he was determined to reshape the American naval officers corps by flooding service with twice the number of midshipmen authorized by Congress:

Young men of good education-parts & connections-we have

29 *Ibid.*, p. 112
30 *Ibid.*, p. 350

never objected to such young men, although they have never been at sea-the more midshipmen of this description, the better the chance of good officers some years hence-those who leave the merchant's service to enter into the navy, especially from the eastward, often wish to return to their first employment, and at times most inconvenient. . . .[31]

Stoddert's strategic direction of the Quasi War during its first year was nearly flawless. He correctly assessed patterns of French privateering activity and American losses, identifying the Caribbean as the major theater of war. After insuring the security of the American coast from invasion and interruption of the nation's trade, Stoddert concentrated all his available resources in the West Indies. He resisted attempts to disperse his limited forces, refusing to send ships into northern waters or to the Old World. By mid-1799 however, the secretary again began to yield to political pressures and plan deployments that would stretch the navy's strength. While the proposed foray of the *United States* and the *Constitution* to Europe would have been a mistake, such political diversions were inevitable.

Stoddert's well conceived plans during the war took into consideration: French activity, British deployments, geography, patterns of trade, prevailing winds, and logistics, and he proved that he could manage ships in time of war, yet the secretary's operation conceptions were marred by a major flaw. Time and again he ignored what Carl von Clausewitz would come to term "friction." Stoddert's plans were usually a bit too neat, too inelastic, based on plans that were overoptimistic. While Stoddert could not be blamed for the primitiveness of the navy's shore-based administration, nor for the less than competent captains under his command (not having the time to produce superior sailors, due to the short period of time that the war lasted), but he was at fault for not factoring into his plans the probable, if inexcusable delays.

A major delay was caused by the navy's inability to man its ships

---

31 Massachusetts Historical Society, Timothy Pickering Papers, Vol. 35, #193

with full crews. Throughout the war, Stoddert found many of his captains still in port weeks after they had been ordered to sea. By the middle of 1799, he had developed a standard rejoinder for dilatory commanders. As an example, he wrote to Captain Christopher Perry that his complement of "220 men. . . .would be a very full crew-perhaps more than necessary. You might with propriety sail 20 or 30 short that number. . . . The *General Greene* must not be delayed a single moment for any additional supply of men."[32]

One questionable operation decision that Stoddert made during the war which also brought him into conflict with President Adams involved captured French sailors. Adams believed that since seamen were so scarce in any navy that "We must sweep the West India seas, and get as many French seamen. . . .whether they are Italians, Spaniards, Germans, or negroes, as we can." The President believed that "seamen are so scarce that they cannot send out large privateers." Through the attrition of French manpower in the Caribbean, Adams held that their warships' activities could be halted. Whether the president knew it or not, Vice Admiral Henry Harvey, commanding the Royal Navy's forces in the Lesser Antilles was pursuing just such a policy with some success.[33]

Stoddert, on the other hand chose to exchange prisoners with the French in the islands. His reasons were practical. First, when the captives were aboard American ships, they consumed a squadron's stores and transporting them to the United States tied down ships, which were always in short supply. Secondly, as secretary of the Board of War during the Revolution, he was in charge of the maintenance of British prisoners, he did want the same burden twenty years later.[34]

In July 1799, Adams was outraged to discover that his navy

32 United States Navy Department, Office of Naval Records and Library, p. 100

33 John Adams, *The Works of John Adams, Second President of the United States; with a Life of the Author*, Charles Francis Adams, ed., 10 vols. (Boston: Little Brown and Company, 1850), VIII, p. 599

34 Kenneth Schaffel, "The American Board of War, 1776-1787" (Ph.D. dissertation, City University of New York, 1938), p. 197

secretary had authorized prisoner exchanges within the Caribbean calling it "one big mistake." If all captives were sent north, Adams reiterated, we shall soon exhaust [Guadeloupe] of seamen. . . . " Despite Adam's insistence, and a clear annunciation of the administration's policy on the part of Stoddert, American commanders remained eager to unload captives as soon as possible. Of the 6,500 prisoners taken during the war, less than 1,000 ever reached the United States.[35]

Complicating the situation in the Caribbean was the condition of Saint-Domingue.[36] The revolution that broke out in France in 1789 inevitably spread to the Caribbean, causing continuous battles that broke out among the different factions such as the liberals against the aristocrats, but mainly the conflicts were between slaves and their masters. Eventually Francois Dominique Toussaint Louverture emerged to lead the war for Saint Domingue's independence.

This situation offered an opportunity for American merchants as neutrals to sail to the country with needed goods, since the newly freed slaves would not deal with the French. It was these merchant ships that were convoyed by Stoddert using the infant United States Navy. The independence of Saint Domingue benefitted the nation in two ways; first, it would weaken French power in the New World, and second it would enrich American merchants. While at first glance, American relations with Saint Domingue would seem to be extremely positive, there were political problems with the Republicans, since many of their leaders were slave owners who believed that the abolition of slavery on the island could spread to America. Additionally, the British opposed outright independence for the same reason. On April 18, 1799, the United States signed an agreement with Louverture that committed him to suppress French privateering and opened Port-au-Prince to free trade with America and Britain.

Early in 1800, there came an imbalance in the American

---

35 United states Navy Department, Office of Naval Records and Library, p. 453

36 Became known as Haiti in 1804.

victories versus the American merchant losses. From January to May, American war ships captured fourteen French privateers and recaptured twenty-four American merchantmen, yet American merchant losses began to mount. The problem was not with the navy, of the twenty-seven ships available during the winter of 1799-1800, twenty-one had been operational in the Caribbean, in March 1800 all but three of the navy's twenty-nine vessels were at sea. The answer to the problem lay with the policies of Great Britain and France.

Even though in November 1799, Napoleon Bonaparte had come to power in France and was agreeable to the idea of improving relations with the United States, the news did not reach the Caribbean, and would not for months, allowing the frequency of French attacks on American shipping to intensify resulting in the capture during a ten week period in the spring of 1800 of thirty-eight American ships.

British naval redeployment also contributed to the American problems in the Caribbean. In July 1798, the British had seventy-one ships in the area, by February 1799, the number had been reduced to thirty-five, and the United States did not have the warships to make up the difference.

Added to this situation was the actions of the *commissair civil* on Guadeloupe, Victor Hugues. Hugues had established a regime on the island that mirrored that of Revolutionary Paris in both its activity and its extremes. As a means of striking at Great Britain after he had captured Guadeloupe from British forces in June 1794, Hugues decided to attack English commerce acting basically as a pirate; collecting fees for the granting of commissions, gaining partial financial control of many pirate ships, and manipulating court decisions to his own benefit. By 1797, he became increasingly antagonistic towards the United States, who were guilty in his mind of supplying British forces in the West Indies and trading with French colonies that were conquered by Britain. Additionally, the French Directory's decrees of 1797 and 1798 permitted a full scale assault on American Caribbean commerce and in the latter year the nearly

100 Yankee ships seized represented about half of Hugues's haul.[37]

In July 1798, Hugues was recalled by the Directory because of his piracy, but returned to the Caribbean in December 1799 as the governor of French Guiana. In this position, he continued his attacks on American commerce.

In addition to supplying convoys for the Caribbean trade, Stoddert now had to again deal with the American merchants who were looking for naval protection on a virtually worldwide basis. By 1789, New England ships had reached Canton with ginseng, beeswax, butter, rum, and sundries, returning with tea. In 1794, Americans opened trade routes to Calcutta and the East Indies. While again Stoddert was eager to do what he could for the commercial community whose political and financial support made the navy possible, but with so few ships available, existing forces had to be concentrated in the Caribbean. The best that Stoddert could offer the merchants was outward protection as far South as the equator.

In the fall of 1799, the merchants took their concerns directly to the President, wanting more than outward bound protection. They had formed their own convoys in the spring for a return from Batavia[38] and asked for naval protection. The president decided that the *Congress* and the *Essex* would leave the United States in January to meet with the convoy. Both ships encountered a gale in the North Atlantic, *Congress* was almost destroyed by the weather, and completely dismasted, limped back to the port of Norfolk,. The *Essex*, also damaged reached Batavia on the 15th of May. Its captain, Edward Preble, put together an American convoy and reached New York City on November 28, 1800.

Even with the almost total loss of the *Congress*, Stoddert again planned a second operation to the Indian Ocean, using two frigates as before. Under the conditions of the Quasi War though, this

---

37 "The Colonial Robespierre': Victor Hugues on Guadeloupe, 1794-1798," *History Today* 27 (November 1977): p. 734-740

38 Present day Jakarta

projected cruise was the most ill-conceived operation of the conflict. As valuable as American trade was with the Orient, it totaled only about 2 percent of all the nation's commerce. Circumstances however defeated the plan-too many warships needed major repairs. The *Congress* dismasted in the Atlantic gale, the *Constellation* dismasted in a night action with *la Vengeance*, and the *Insurgent* buffeted by a storm over Cuba, and carrying a deficient British made foremast, leaving none for service beyond the Caribbean.

In 1800, the British began to step up their searches, seizures, and impressments and as a consequence even Alexander Hamilton grew concerned when he came to realize the seriousness of British depredations. Stoddert too, took note. He hoped that diplomacy would head off a break in relations, but he wrote to Thomas Fitzsimons,[39]" We ought not however to rely solely on this, when we have the means of protecting our commerce from the lawless ravages of British privateers in our own hands."Obviously the secretary of the navy was not an anglophile.[40]

But the problem of dealing with increasing British spoliations would fall to succeeding administrations. For Stoddert there remained the war with France, although there was now the possibility of peace with France because of the change in diplomacy in Paris with the ascension to power of Napoleon. Nevertheless, while he advised his captains not to seek encounters with French national warships, they were also not to "avoid engagements with them, should they show a disposition to attack." Pirates were to be treated as before, but American men-of-war were to be employed "more in convoying our trade than formally-and of course, less in cruising." Stoddert was ordering his captains to go over to the defensive, unless the French became as active as before, in which case, they were to resume their normal operations.[41]

---

39 Philadelphia merchant and Congressman

40 United States Navy Department, Office of Naval Records and Library, p. 518-519

41 *Ibid.*, p. 536-537

Stoddert learned of the Convention of Mortefontaine, the treaty ending the Quasi War on December 13, 1800, he spread the news to his captains, but also ordered them to continue to provide escorts for the merchant convoys and to halt hostilities unless the French unexpectedly continued their attacks.

The navy's last battle of the Quasi War came off Havana. French privateering, which had virtually come to an end was renewed. Stoddert immediately ordered three warships to the Cuba station, where the American ships quickly drove off the privateers. Stoddert's final problem concerned not the French, but disease. Captain Timothy Newman of the *Warren* violated one of Stoddert's principal policies: commanders were not to remain in port for extended periods in the West Indies. The eleven days that Newman spent in Havana cost the lives of forty-two crew members including Newman and his son from yellow fever.

Newman's foolishness and insubordination infuriated both Adams and Stoddert. The secretary would have called for a court-martial if Newman had not "escaped by death."

The loss of the presidency by John Adams spelled both a personal and political disappointment to Stoddert. Not that he hoped to stay on in his position as secretary of the navy, an Adams victory would have allowed him to resign, now, he would have to stay on until Jefferson was inaugurated. Jefferson however asked him to stay on until a replacement could be found, which finally occurred on April 30, 1801. The American naval operations of the Quasi War had come to an end.

Chapter 6

The End of the Quasi War – The Negotiations

T he Convention of 1800 ended the Quasi War between France and the United States and settled the dispute over neutral rights which had marked the period of the Directory. It also removed the causes of irritation which had arisen under the treaties of 1778. By its provisions, the United States secured a release from the one and only entangling alliance in her history. For France, the convention marked the first successful step in the general pacification inaugurated by Napoleon Bonaparte upon his accession to power.

The publication of the X.Y.Z. dispatches in the United States in 1798 so alarmed Talleyrand, then France's secretary for foreign affairs that he began to agitate for peace with America.[1] Talleyrand continued this policy when Napoleon assumed control of France, and he deserves the principal credit for the restoration of normal relations between the two countries.

Both sides looked for an end to hostilities. The French at the time were engaged in a war with the Second Coalition[2] and did not

---

1 Talleyrand believed that France had everything to lose and nothing to gain from a declared war with the United States. The safety of her commerce, the future of her colonies, and the interests of her allies dictated a policy of peace. This was especially true in regards to the West Indian colonies of France that were dependent on the Yankee merchant.

2 An alliance composed of England, Turkey, Austria, and Russia

want a neutral United States drawn in on either side; a belligerent America allied with France would see its shipping attacked by the British navy, while a neutral America would be able to supply the French with desperately need grain. The United States, for the same reasons wished to remain neutral.

One of Talleyrand's first acts in December 1799, was a statement of France's position vis-a- vis the United States. It was of prime importance, he said that France return to her natural relations with the American government. The death of George Washington[3] offered an excellent opportunity to inform the French people of the approaching change in Franco-American relations. A giant ceremony was held in the Temple of Mars, and an eloquent funeral oration pronounced, the speaker making full use of his opportunity to also praise the great man who had become ruler of France.[4]

The American government failed to show a similar zeal for beginning any negotiations. It continued to declare the treaties of 1778 null and void and refused to stop its retaliatory measures against French armed vessels. In spite of the Federalist attitude towards France, Adams decided to send three more ministers to Paris. The meeting began in Paris on April 2, 1800.

Talleyrand instructed the French ministers to consider the negotiations from the point of view of the past, the present, and the future. With regard to the past, the American ministers should have it pointed out to them that their country owed a great debt to France because of the French aid during their Revolution. For the present, the aim should be to end the commercial depredations and bad feeling between the two countries. But most attention should be given to the future. The objectives that France pursued in 1778 were still valid: separate the then colonies, now the United States from England, deprive England of the raw materials produced by America, add to the security of the French and Spanish colonies,

---

3   December 14, 1799

4   Napoleon

encourage American trade with France and her colonies, attach the United States to France politically, arouse rivalries between England and America, and finally, secure the advantage of American affinity towards France in future wars.

The French representatives were told that they should follow two principles in the negotiations: Re-establish the treaties and conventions in place before the current hostilities and demand a revision of the treaties so that France would enjoy the advantages accorded England by Jay's treaty. If this could be accomplished, the only issue remaining would be the question of damages. Talleyrand believed that the injuries claimed by one or the other of the two countries would be one of the following: damages to French colonies in default of United States guarantees under the existing treaties; damages to French colonies through the stopping of commerce by American warships; and damage to Americans from French warships. Despite the listing of French losses, Talleyrand admitted that the Americans would claim greater damages and that they would be justified: "The irregularity, the political injustice of our legislation on privateering, and the violent manner of its execution by our corsairs and our courts lead us to believe that their [the Americans'] argument is well founded." But he believed that recent statements of the President of the United States and the conversations of several American ministers showed that the American government did not expect an exact or immediate payment. [5]

The American ministers however, were instructed to state at the beginning of the negotiations that the United States considered compensation for the losses of her citizens at the hands of French vessels or agents as "an indispensable condition of the treaty." Another problem was the regulation of navigation and commerce. Articles XVII and XXII of the 1778 treaty between the United States and France, which permitted each nation to take its prizes to the ports of the other and forbade the outfitting in their ports of privateers

---

5   E. Wilson Lyon, "The Franco-American Convention of 1800," *The Journal of Modern History*, Vol. XII, Sept. 1940, Number 3, p. 313

belonging to the enemy of either nation, had caused a great deal of difficulty, and the United States opposed renewing these articles. Also, a renewal was impossible as long as Jay's treaty was in effect because in Articles XXIV and XXV of that document, the United States had agreed to forbid the arming of privateers of Britain's enemies in her ports and to deny shelter or refuge to prizes captured from Great Britain. And since the United States had abrogated its treaties with France, the Jay treaty took precedence. In addition to the payment of claims, there were also several other points that the Americans were instructed to make: first, that treaties voided by Congress were not to be revived in whole or in part, though the essence of a voided treaty might be part of a new treaty; second, "No guarantee of the whole or any part of the dominions of France [was to] be stipulated nor any engagement made, in the nature of an alliance;" Third, aids or loans "in any form whatsoever," any engagement inconsistent with a private treaty, especially Jay's treaty, and privileges or powers to consuls "incompatible with complete sovereignty of the United States" were forbidden; Finally, the new treaty was to be singed for a period of twelve years.[6]

Pursuant to their instructions, the Americans first raised the question of damages due their fellow citizens, so the initial negotiations turned on this point alone. To avoid this topic, the French began the talks with a proposal that it was first necessary to establish "the rules and the mode of procedure for indemnification of those injuries for which the two nations, respectively, may have demands against each other."[7] This raised the question of nation claims, whereas the Americans were primarily interested in the damages due individuals. They believed that the adjudication of national claims would be extremely difficult.

---

6 Instructions to the American ministers, William Vans Murray, Oliver Ellsworth, and William Richardson, October 22, 1800, American state papers, foreign relations (Washington, 1832,II, p. 307 (hereafter these papers will be referred to as "A.S.P., For.rel.")

7 American ministers to French ministers, April 7, 1800, and French ministers to American ministers, April 8, 1800, *Ibid.* II, p. 314

The French then attempted to embarrass the Americans by asking them if the laws passed by Congress suspending commerce with France had been lifted as the French laws aimed at the United States had been, knowing full well that the American laws had not been suspended but in fact extended until March 3, 1801. The Americans answered lamely that as the acts were retaliatory, they would disappear with France's removal of the original irritation.

In spite of the French machinations, the Americans clung tenaciously to the idea of first settling the indemnity due the citizens of the United States. Their proposal was a framework for handling the claims. A commission of five was to be selected to sit in Paris and examine each individual case; two members were to be nominated by each nation and these four were to select a fifth. Any three members were qualified to conduct the commission's business, provided both countries were represented. Injured parties were to be allowed two years in which to submit their petitions, and the settlements were to be made three months after the decision paid in 6 percent bonds, one third redeemable in gold or silver in three years, another third in five years, and the final third in seven years. Claims against the United states were to be paid in Washington under the same conditions, but six months after the award.[8] The French ministers agreed to compensation, but maintained that it was part of the old treaty (1778) and should be laid aside until the new treaty had been made. The American ministers replied that they were not empowered to make a new treaty before the claims had been settled.[9]

The negotiations made little progress during May and June, Napoleon was engaged in his second Italian campaign and Talleyrand was ill.. On May 17, the Americans wrote to Secretary of State Pickering that, "Our success is doubtful."[10] The main problem for the French however was had the American refused to move beyond the issue of the claims and also that the former treaties would not be

---

8   American ministers to French ministers, April 21, 1800, p. 465

9   American ministers to French ministers, May 8, 1800

10 A.S.P., For.rel, II, p. 325

recognized.

By the end of May, it became clear that the French ministers would need new instructions if the negotiations were to proceed. They sent a lengthy report to Talleyrand raising two points, first, were the treaties really abrogated? And second, did France need the old treaties? The French ministers believed that the answer to the first question was no, that only a declared war could abrogate a treaty, but if they used that argument then the Americans would have to consult Washington which would delay the talks for months. In answer to the second question, they believed that French interests would suffer little if the treaties were annulled since the privilege of outfitting privateers and bringing prizes to American ports was never used because France wished to keep the United States neutral. In signing a new commercial treaty, France need only insist that she be put on the same basis as Great Britain in regard to privileges in American ports. Finally they told Talleyrand, if the 1778 treaties were annulled, it would mean that France would have the right to oppose paying indemnities to American citizens, since by abrogating them the United States would be cancelling any rights they conferred, including paying claims. As such the French ministers recommended that Talleyrand instruct them to make a new treaty with the United States.[11]

The talks now reached another stopping point because Talleyrand had to communicate with Napoleon who was still in Italy about the status of the negotiations. Talleyrand informed him that the talks had reached a deadlock and that up to this point, France had accepted the principle of indemnity for the losses to American private citizens and that he (Talleyrand) believed that if the old treaties were cancelled, the debts would also be cancelled.

While waiting for instructions from their government the French ministers attempted to make some new proposals. They receded slightly from their former position of "old treaties with

---

11   French ministers to Talleyrand, May 26, 1800

indemnities, or new treaties with indemnities." Now they suggested that for a period of seven years France might have the option of accepting changes in the treaties or of paying the indemnities. Finally, the French proposed that the United States relinquish her claim to indemnities and then France would renounce the privileges of Article XI of the treaty of alliance which guaranteed the French colonies in America.[12]

On July 11, the American ministers made a new proposal, what they called a "moment of conference." They asked the French ministers to write down all the points of difference between the two countries; the minister of the United States would then consider them as quickly as possible and then ask for a verbal conference, thus obviating longs delays. The French accepted the suggestion readily and prepared a list of disputed issues.

Before any action could be taken on the points of difference, a change in the American cabinet and American public opinion took place. Timothy Pickering had been replaced as secretary of state by John Marshall and Republican success in state elections meant that possibly Thomas Jefferson could defeat John Adams in the next presidential election.

Talleyrand's reaction to this news showed that he had a clear perception of American public opinion and also that it could be the basis of a future path for French policy:

His accession should bring the United States back to us, but we should not forget that we have improved our position by moderation and by complete non-intervention in their internal affairs.[13] We can

---

12 French ministers to American ministers, June 20 -July 19, 1800, It is interesting to note that 21/2 months later, the French reclaimed the Louisiana territory from Spain under the Third Treaty of San Ildefonso.

13 Apparently, Talleyrand had learned his lesson after attempting to influence the Adams/Jefferson election in 1796 by having the French ambassador to the United States, Pierre Adet openly support Thomas Jefferson, even to the point of implying that if Jefferson was not elected there could be war between the two countries.

make Mr. Jefferson's administration effective only by proving that we do not desire to abuse his partiality for us and by renouncing the expectation of sacrifices and condescensions which would give his policy a character it should not be allowed to assume. Mr. Jefferson will consider it a duty to unite around him all true Americans and to resume with full force the system of balance between France and England which alone is wise for the United States. This policy accords best with our own interests. We have nothing to desire in the United States except to see them prosper. Without agitation, without intrigue, jealousy of England and her demands will lead them to a rapprochement with us.

It is my opinion that we should see [in the recent news] new motives for terminating our quarrels and for ending them generously. I am persuaded that it is our liberality and conciliation that has produced the division in the cabinet and in the nation. Not to persist in this policy is to run the risk of uniting all the parties against us and of justifying all the aggressive measures followed up to the present day.[14]

The possible change in American leadership also affected the American ministers. Talleyrand believed that they now wished to end the negotiations in such a way that both countries would benefit, therefore he suggested to Napoleon that France should reply in the affirmative to the American minister's last proffer by attempting to prove that the 1778 treaties were not abrogated and that France could sacrifice any unfair advantages that she possessed provided that her rights were not inferior to any other nation. Also at this point, Talleyrand was enjoying a period of popularity in the United States as opposed to denunciation heaped upon him at the time of the X.Y.Z. affair. Joseph Letombe, the French Consul General in the United States wrote to Talleyrand telling him that the Republicans were calling him "their savior" and saying that without his "prudence, calmness, wise and prescient policy, and his generous sacrifice of his personal "griefs" against Secretary of State Pickering their country

---

14 Talleyrand's report to Napoleon, July 13, 1800

would have been French two years ago.[15]

On July 25, Talleyrand urged a conclusion of the negotiations. He proposed that France declare peremptorily that she was "resolved to make all the sacrifices friendship demanded, that the principle of indemnities had been agreed to and would be respected," but that America could not denounce her treaties with France unilaterally. While he was preparing this report, he received a letter from the French commissioners enclosing a proposal from the American ministers with a change in the payment of the indemnities agreed to by France. The indemnities now would not be paid until the United States could offer an article to the eventual agreement stipulating free entry into the ports of the two countries warships and prizes of each nation, to the exclusion of their enemies. Furthermore, the indemnities would not be paid unless the United States could offer such an article within seven years.[16]

Napoleon approved the suggestion of the Americans that France be put on equal terms with Great Britain in the right of taking her prizes into American ports, but now refused to pay indemnities to American citizens.

With this action on the part of Napoleon, France now openly declared that in protracting the discussions, the aim was to avoid paying the indemnities. As Talleyrand wrote to the French ministers: "You will see, Citizen Ministers, that we hope as much as possible to set the indemnities aside." If it were absolutely necessary to pay them, the payments should be arranged in as small amounts as possible and for as remote a date as possible.[17]

Both parties then deviated again from their original positions. Talleyrand decided that a new treaty would be necessary and submitted one to Napoleon. It was a statesmanlike document which

---

15 Letombe to Talleyrand, Philadelphia, July 15, 1800

16 American ministers to French ministers, July 23, 1800; French ministers to Talleyrand, July 27, 1800

17 Talleyrand to French ministers, August 5, 1800

treated the Franco-American dispute in a world significant context. France would continue her traditional role as the protector of neutral commerce, but not accept the American proposal of sacrificing the principle of "free ships, free goods." Talleyrand's interest in neutral shipping did not arise from a love of the United States, but from an appreciation of the value of neutral commerce to France in time of war. An armed neutrality was being organized in northern Europe against British interference with trade, and the minister did not consider it advisable to depart from principles which had made France so many friends in the period of the American Revolution. On the question of prizes, France should be placed on the same basis as Great Britain. There could be no discussion of any other possibilities. On their part, the American ministers saw the possibility of having to make concessions to the French, because of their steadfastness in support of their positions, and so communicated with the secretary of state:

It has, however, become manifest, that the negotiations must be abandoned, or our instructions deviated from. Should the latter be ventured upon, which, from present appearances, is not improbable, the deviation will be no greater than a change of circumstances may be presumed to justify.[18]

"The change of circumstances" was the great improvement in the position of France due to her victories in Italy and her friendly overtures to Russia and the Scandinavian nations.

At the same time, the American government was becoming irked by the long delay in negotiations , which it had expected to see completed by April 1.[19] In reply, Marshall wrote to President Adams on August 25 that he would not be surprised if another month went by without the signing of a treaty. Adams wrote back asking "whether the President ought not at the opening of the season to recommend to Congress an immediate and general declaration of war against

18 To Secretary of State Pickering, August 15, 1800, A.S.P., For. rel., p. 333

19 Andrew J. Montague, "John Marshall," *The American Secretaries of State and their diplomacy,* ed. Samuel Flagg Bemis (New York: Alfred J. Knopf, 1927), II, p. 253-254

the French Republic." Fortunately, Marshall counseled a moderate course without recourse to hostilities.

At the end of August, both sides once again put forth new proposals. To the French alternative, "old treaties and indemnities or a new treaty without indemnities," the Americans responded with the following new ideas: Declare the former treaties renewed except in so far as they are changed by the present treaty; Allow a seven year period in which either party, by the payment of 3,000,000 francs, might reduce the rights of the other, as to privateers and prizes, to those of the most favored nation; The mutual guarantees in Article XI[20] of the Treaty of Alliance (1778) should be so specified and limited that the obligation resting on France would be the delivery of military stores in her own ports to the value of a million dollars, and for the United States the delivery in her own ports of provisions to the value of a million dollars; Furthermore, either party might be given the privilege of freeing itself from this obligation by the payment of 5,000,000 francs within seven years. Articles of the Treaty of Amity and Commerce (1778) except Article XVII[21] should be made to conform to the most favored nation principle. Indemnities were to be paid by the two nations for the claims of individuals. Ships taken on either side were to be returned or paid for, and property seized and not yet condemned was to be restored to its owners.

The French ministers contended that the proposal to modify Article XVII meant that the United States was offering a new treaty instead of a re-establishment of the old ones, and that, therefore, no indemnities were due. They then made their proposals. Complete re-establishment of the old treaties; the nomination of two commissions to liquidate the damages suffered by each country; changes to Articles XVII and XXII[22] which, after seven years, would put France on an

---

20 Article XI" The two Parties mutually from the present time and forever, against all other powers. . . .

21 Article XVII "And that more effectual Care may be taken for the Security of the Subjects and inhabitants of both Parties, that they suffer no injury by men of War or Privateers of the other Party. . . .

22 Article XXII "For the better promoting of Commerce on both sides. . . .

equal footing with Great Britain in American ports, and a provision that the guarantee of Article XI could be converted into a loan of 2,000,000 francs in time of need. But no indemnities were to be paid by France if Articles XVII and XXII were not established in their entirety. The American reply:

> Having exhausted their efforts to discover, by a spirit of justice and accommodation, the means of accomplishing the desires and realizing the views of both nations, [they] can only hope to avail themselves of the better directed efforts of the ministers plenipotentiary with whom they have the honor to treat.[23]

Additionally, the American ministers repeated a proposal they made three days previously in which they suggested that the United States be given the option , if she chose, of exonerating herself from her obligation under Article XI of the Treaty of Alliance and from French rights under Articles XVII and XXII of the Treaty of Amity and Commerce, within seven years by paying 8,000,000 francs.[24] The French answer to this proposal was an offer to relinquish their privileges under the three articles if the United States would assume the responsibility for paying the damages claimed by its own citizens. The French reasoning in making this proposal was to avoid the problem of indemnities not by creating commissions for settling them, but to leave each government free to settle the subject of indemnities with its own nationals as it chose, after the treaty was concluded. This, the French believed would be comparable to the situation after the signing of a treaty ending a war. Two days later, the Americans responded. The greatest concession that they could make would be a provision that stated "if at the exchange of ratifications the United States shall propose a mutual relinquishment of indemnities, the French Republic will agree to the same; and in such case, the former treaties shall not be deemed obligatory."[25]

---

23 American ministers to French ministers

24 *Ibid.*

25 For the ministers plenipotentiary of the French Republic, September 6, 1800

At this point, the negotiations reached a deadlock. Joseph Bonaparte, Napoleon's brother and one of the French negotiators stated that he would resign rather than sign a treaty accepting a modification of the treaties of 1778 and still providing for indemnities to American citizens.[26] The French now awaited the next move by the Americans, after a sharp exchange of opinions on September 12.

The next day, the American ministers, Ellsworth, Davie, and Murray proposed a temporary settlement which would permit a restoration of normal political and commercial relations.

The ministers plenipotentiary of the respective parties not being able at present to agree respecting the former treaties and indemnities, the parties will, in due and convenient time, further treat on these subjects; and until they shall have agreed respecting the same, the said treaties shall have no operation.[27]

When the French received this message, a conference of the two commissions was arranged for September 19. This principle of a temporary agreement was readily accepted by the French, and the ministers of both nations then moved rapidly to a settlement of the issues. A document was drafted treating matters previously covered in the treaties of 1778. In the end the settlement was more comprehensive than the American ministers intended. The French agreed not to require American ships to carry any papers other than those customary in the United States. The Americans finally consented to allowing privateers of both countries access to each other's ports and accorded them most-favored-nation status.

Talleyrand's plan for continuance of the liberal measures of the 1778 treaties was accepted by the Americans, France also advocated continuing the principles of "free ships, free goods." Additionally, the French suggested freedom of convoys and their exception from visit if the commander of the convoy reported that no ships were transporting contraband, and a liberal definition of commerce. The

26 A.S.P., For. rel., II, p. 338

27 American ministers to French ministers, September 13, 1800

insertion of these provisions was not only for the American, but was also expected to win the friendship of the maritime powers of northern Europe. This policy represented a reversal of the Directory's measures and a return to France's historic position regarding human rights. The question of indemnifications, a major point for the Americans, was left to be resolved later. In fact, reparations were specifically excluded from the document:

Article V, Convention of Mortefontaine:

The debts contracted by one of the two nations, with individuals of the other, or by the individuals of one, with the individuals of the other shall be paid, or the payment shall be prosecuted in the same manner, as if there had been no misunderstanding between the two States. *But this clauseshall not extend to indemnities claimed on account of captures, or confiscations.*[28]

Some irritation arose over the question of a title for the document. The French desired to call it a "treaty of amity and commerce" and to make it more than a temporary agreement, the Americans however opposed this terminology stating that they had consented to negotiate only on the basis of a "convention." When the French ministers disagreed, the Americans said that they were willing to discuss the substance of a treaty and to call the document "a provisional treaty."The French consented, realizing that further insistence would involve delays and perhaps imperil the negotiations. The next debate came over the language that the document should be written in, the Americans wanted to have it in both languages. The French agreed on the condition that the French copy would be declared the original, which followed the precedent of the Treaty of Alliance of 1778, which was signed in two languages, but was declared to have been prepared in French.

The last changes in the treaty were made at the suggestion of Napoleon. He wished to have the title changed from "provisional treaty to "convention" and that the conclusion of the convention

---

28 My italics

be in the name of the First Consul of the French Republic[29] and the president of the United States. In return for these alterations, the Americans were given the privilege of stating that the treaty had been signed in both languages.

Talleyrand approved of the work that the French ministers did on the treaty:

> You have rendered a real service to the French nation and to its government by putting an end to the misunderstanding which deprived France of one of the most important branches of its commercial communications and by re-establishing between the two peoples that good will and attachment which nothing should have altered.[30]

The American ministers believed that the convention was as advantageous for the United States as for France. As the ministers wrote, it would have been foolish to have "left the United States involved in a contest, and according to appearances, soon alone in a contest, which it might be as difficult for them to relinquish with honor as to pursue with a prospect of advantage."[31]

Talleyrand immediately took steps to see that the French administration acted in the spirit of the reconciliation. He worked to see that no vessel was condemned in violation of the principle of "free ships, free goods" while the French government was awaiting ratification by the United States. (France had promised to pay for any ships seized contrary to this part of the agreement in the period of time between the signing and the ratification of the convention.) He also urged the minister to execute the terms of the convention at once in the French colonies. Some of them, such as St. Domingue, were virtually allied with the United States, while others, like Guadeloupe and Guiana were tied to France. Talleyrand knew that the French warships in these areas must immediately cease

---

29 Napoleon Bonaparte

30 Talleyrand to the French ministers, September 27, 1800

31 To the secretary of state, A.S.P.,

attacking American ships or peace between the two nations would be impossible. Additionally, on October 10, the minister of the French navy was ordered to free any American vessels that were detained in French ports.

To begin commercial operations with the United States, Talleyrand instructed French commercial agents in America to begin work setting up new business relationships that would go into effect as soon as the convention was ratified. To further assist in reestablishing trading relations, Talleyrand replaced Joseph Letombe as French Consul General with Louis Andre Pichon, then head of the second division of the foreign office. Talleyrand considered him to be an excellent fit for the position:

This citizen is well known in the United States, where he has served the Republic as secretary to two successive legations. He knows perfectly the persons and interests of the states and the lines which unite these interests to those of France. This information is combined with great wisdom and a conciliatory character ideally suited to assure the execution of the measures of union and conciliation which the First Consul had adopted toward the United States.[32]

Pichon's first mission was to insure that American ship's were not being attacked in the Caribbean and to make the American government aware of Talleyrand's orders to have the attacks cease. Talleyrand's advice to the new consul was a model of wisdom. He should apply himself to dissipating all suspicion or mistrust of France by "avoiding meddling in local questions and by affecting no marked personal preference in his relations with the influential persons of one or the other party." He was to recommend the same conduct to all French persons including officials, residing in the United States.[33]

The most reassuring factor in Franco-American relations was the election of Thomas Jefferson as president in 1800. Pichon

---

32 Report to the First Consul, October 17, 1800

33 Supplement d'instructions pour le Cit. Pichon Cr General de relat.com. auxEtatsUnis, brumaire an 9 [October 23-November21, 1800

received the most cordial greetings from the new president and the members of his administration. He was told that American warships had been recalled and that instructions had gone out to American agents in French colonies to close down their activities there. Since the law suspending all commerce With France expired on March 3, 1801, the American government discontinued all the retaliatory measures passed during President Adams administration. As France had already suspended all her decrees against American commerce, the two countries were returning to normal relations even before the convention had been ratified. Jefferson went a step further and appointed Robert R. Livingston, of New York, as minister to France. At the same time Consul Pichon worked on the return of French prisoners and the resumption of commercial relations.

Before the treaty could be discussed in the American Senate, problems arose on the French side. The French ministers saw no objection to limiting the duration of the treaty to eight years , but now did not believe that France should allow the pure and simple abolition of the treaties of 1778, which would result from expunging Article II.

Article II, Treaty of Mortefontaine:

The Ministers Plenipotentiary of the two Parties, not being able to agree at present respecting the Treaty of Alliance of 6th February, 1778, the Treaty of Amity and Commerce of the same date, and the . . . Convention of 14th November 1788, nor upon the indemnities, mutually due, or claimed, the Parties will negotiate further on these subjects at a convenient time, and until they may have agreed upon these points, the said Treaties, and . . . .Convention shall have no operation, and the relations of the two Countries shall be regulated as follows.

Furthermore, by the American ratification, France would still be liable for the indemnities. The French ministers now wished to remove Article II only on condition that the United States renounce the indemnities, which brought the discussion back to where it

159

had been months earlier.[34] Talleyrand agreed with the ministers and reported back to Napoleon with two suggestions: first, open new negotiations with the Americans, who since they would have to receive new instructions would take time, or second, give a conditional ratification. Talleyrand suggested the second alternative, stating that the First Consul ratify the convention, with the expunging of Article II providing that the United States agree to abandon the indemnities.[35]

Talleyrand was also interested in keeping the original convention because of the favorable effect it had on French foreign policy. He wrote to Napoleon:

> It is not without interest for the honor and policy adopted by the government of the Republic to preserve the first treaty, in which liberal principles on the laws of neutrality have been generously and voluntarily stipulated by France. The rules which this treaty consecrates have not been without influence on the efforts which have been made in the North to free neutrality from the yoke of England. This consideration assures the convention of September 30 an honorable place in the history of international law.[36]

In order to influence neutral nations, Talleyrand published the terms of the convention almost immediately after it had been signed.[37] At that point, the discussions ceased because both Talleyrand and Napoleon became ill. Finally Talleyrand returned and immediately began to push the negotiations agreeing to a ratification of the convention and to a limitation of the convention to eight years, provided the American government would interpret the expunging

---

34 The American position was to abolish the entangling 1778 treaties and also receive the indemnities.

35 Report to the First Consul, June 22, 1801

36 *Ibid.*

37 The reason the French gave for publishing the document as they told the Americans however was the desire to inform French agents immediately of the new relations with the United States

of Article II as a "reciprocal renunciation of the representative pretensions which are the object of the said article." that is, treaties and indemnities.[38] The American accepted on July 31, 1801.

While the American ministers were carrying on negotiations with the French ministers and with Talleyrand, the French power rested with Napoleon Bonaparte. In the fall of 1797, Napoleon massed an army at Boulogne in northern France to invade Britain, but after surveying the Channel waters, he deemed the project all but impossible without a much larger naval force to occupy the entire Channel to prevent destruction of his troop ships before they could reach England."To carry out a descent on England without mastery of the sea would be the boldest and most difficult operation ever undertaken,"[39] Napoleon declared.

Instead of risking a costly and potentially bloody assault on England, Napoleon decided to isolate her from her sources of colonial wealth by conquering Malta and Egypt which would cut England's Mediterranean routes to India, insisting that "In order truly to destroy England, we must occupy Egypt."[40]

As Napoleon arrived in Egypt after taking Malta, his forces was followed by a British fleet under the command of Sir Horatio Nelson. From August first to third, there ensued a major naval battle at Aboukir Bay on the Mediterranean coast off the Nile Delta of Egypt.[41] The result of the battle was a major victory for the British forces.

As the aura of French invincibility disintegrated, conquered peoples began a rebellion against Napoleon across Europe, in the Caribbean, a slave uprising all but stripped the French of authority on Saint Domingue and cut the vital flow of sugar to France. Napoleon's

---

38 *Ibid.*

39 Felix Maurice Hippiel Markham, *Napoleon* (New York: The New American Library of World Literature, 1963), p. 44

40 *Ibid.* p. 42

41 Also known as The Battle of the Nile

answer to the situation was to look West, which meant supporting Talleyrand in the peace talks with the United States, because renewal of Franco-American trade was paramount, but he also needed to end the Quasi War that had disrupted vital French commerce with her islands in the Caribbean. If the talks were successful the United States would no longer be an enemy of France, but rather a neutral nation supporting freedom of the seas as espoused by the Second League of Armed Neutrality.[42]

On September 31, 1800, Napoleon signed a secret treaty with Spain that returned Louisiana to France in return for Etruria (now Tuscany and part of Umbria). By exchanging Louisiana for Etruria, the Spanish king ridded himself of a costly American colony. The Spanish monarch boasted of exchanging "vast wilderness of the Mississippi and Missouri. . . .for the classical land of the arts and science. . ."[43]

For Napoleon however, acquiring Louisiana gave him control of commerce on the Mississippi River and a huge territory[44]that he envisioned developing as a bountiful granary for France and her West Indian Islands. His problem was even though Spain had ruled Louisiana since 1763, they did not populate the area, which created a huge vacuum that Americans willingly filled. By 1800, American farmers, hunters, and merchants had settled the Ohio valley, the Illinois territory and upper Louisiana. The Mississippi River was

---

42 The Second League of Armed Neutrality was an alliance of the northern European naval powers; Denmark, Norway, Prussia, Sweden, and Russia whose aim was to protect neutral shipping against the British Royal Navy's wartime policy of unlimited search of neutral shipping for French contraband, in an attempt to cut off military supplies and other trade to the French Republic. The British government considered the League a form of alliance with France.

43 Alexander DeConde, *This Affair of Louisiana* (New York: Charles Scribner's Sons, 1976), p. 96

44 To put the area of Louisiana in perspective, its territory included land that formed fifteen states: Arkansas, Missouri, Iowa, Oklahoma, Kansas, and Nebraska. Also parts of: Minnesota, North Dakota, South Dakota, New Mexico, Texas, Montana, Wyoming, Colorado, Louisiana, and the Canadian provinces of Alberta and Saskatchewan.

clogged with hundreds of flatboats carrying whiskey, flour, and produce to New Orleans. The heavy river traffic had swelled the river town into a prosperous port city for trade between the area and the rest of the world. Secretary of State James Madison described the importance of the Mississippi as "the Hudson, the Delaware, the Potomac, and all the navigable rivers of the Atlantic states, formed into one stream."[45]

Three thousand ships a year passed through New Orleans, more than half of them flying American colors. American merchants in eastern states financed and controlled more than half the port's commerce, and the rural areas beyond New Orleans. Americans made up more than half of the white population, owned vast sugar and cotton plantations, and raised huge herds of cattle on lands stretching from Louisiana to Texas. The tide of American migrants had submerged Spain's influence and threatened her sovereignty in Texas and even Mexico. Rumors of French army landings in Louisiana united Americans as they had not been since the War of Independence. "Every eye in the U.S.," President Jefferson noted, "is now fixed on this affair of Louisiana. Perhaps nothing since the revolutionary war has produced more uneasy sensations through the body of the nation."[46] The French were aware of the apprehension of the American government towards the situation in Louisiana, "I am afraid they [the Americans] may strike at Louisiana before we can take it over."[47]

To the consternation of the French government, as President, Jefferson began to lose his love of France. "There is on the globe, one single spot, the possessor of which is our natural enemy. It is New Orleans, through which the produce of three-eighths of our territory must pass to market. The day that France takes possession of New Orleans fixes the sentence which is to restrain her forever within her

45 Madison to Senator Charles Pinckney, November 27, 1802

46 Thomas Jefferson to American secretary for foreign affairs Robert Livingston, April 18, 1802

47 Pichon to Talleyrand, October 15, 1801

low water mark. From that moment we must marry ourselves to the British fleet and nation."[48]

Napoleon, undeterred, began putting plans in motion to move troops to Louisiana. In August 1802, he told Talleyrand that, "my intention is that we take possession of Louisiana with the least possible delay, that this expedition be made in the greatest secrecy, and that it have the appearance of being directed to St. Domingue."[49]To this end, he positioned 20,000 French troops in Dunkerque[50]awaiting transport to Louisiana, but a slave rebellion in Saint Domingue had unexpectedly evolved into a costly guerrilla war that forced Napoleon to divert supplies and ships from the Louisiana expedition. The war ended with control of the island in the hands of Toussaint L'Ouverture. While he stopped short of declaring independence, L' Ouverture nevertheless assumed political control and opened what had been an exclusive preserve to American and British commerce as a gesture of gratitude for their help in the seven year rebellion. In an attempt to regain control, Napoleon sent his brother-in-law General Charles Victor Emanuel Leclerc to Saint Domingue. Leclerc offered Toussaint and the slaves freedom under French rule, if Toussaint pledged allegiance to France. When Toussaint agreed, Leclerc promptly arrested him and sent him to prison in France where he died a months later.

Infuriated by the deception, the island's slaves descended on the French army hacking their way through the French lines with machetes and knives until 10,000 French troops lay dead and mutilated. Additionally, swarms of mosquitoes infected the remaining soldiers with yellow fever, until by the end of September 1802, 24,000 French lives including General Leclerc were lost. To retain sovereignty over the island, Napoleon had no choice but to

---

48 Jefferson to French diplomat Pierre du Pont de Nemours, Paul Leicester Ford, *The Writings of Thomas Jefferson* (New York: Putnam, 1892-1899, 10 vols.), p. 363

49 Alexander DeConde, This Affair of Louisiana, p. 111

50 Dunkirk

delay the Louisiana expedition and sent reinforcements to Saint Domingue.

The growing tension between Napoleon and the United States coupled with the amount of Americans flocking into New Orleans began to have an effect on the Spanish authorities who decided to revoke the American Right of Deposit[51], fearing that they would lose control of the city. This action caused the Americans to consider force of arms to reclaim their privileges. "We would be justified to ourselves and to the world in taking possession of the port in question and reclaiming, by force of arms, the advantages of which we have been unjustly deprived."[52]And from Secretary of State James Madison, "There are now or in less than two years will not be less than 200,000 militia on the waters of the Mississippi . . . .[who] would march at a moment's warning to remove obstructions from that outlet to the sea . . .every man regards the free use of the river as a natural and indefensible right and is conscious of the physical force that at any time give effect to it."[53]

Toward the end of 1802, President Jefferson attempted two approaches to solve the problem. First, he began to prepare for war by sending troops to Fort Adams, located in Mississippi, and buying as much land as possible from the Indian tribes along the east bank of the Mississippi River. Secondly, he sent James Monroe to Paris to buy New Orleans and Florida.

The possible war frenzy frightened the Spanish ambassador in Washington. He warned Madrid that if Spain did not restore the American right of deposit in New Orleans "the impulse of public opinion . . . will force the President and Republicans to declare

---

51 The right to transfer cargo from one ship to another without paying port fees. The U.S. negotiated this right at New Orleans (which was a Spanish port at the time) in the Pinckney Treaty of 1792. E.g., moving cargo from a flat boat to an outbound cargo ship. It was a valuable concession.

52 *Charleston Courier*, January 11, 1803

53 Alexander DeConde, *This Affair of Louisiana*, p. 124

war."[54]At Napoleon's insistence, Spain yielded allowing Jefferson a diplomatic victory.

Delays in obtaining enough ships for the Louisiana expedition forced Napoleon to transfer his army from Dunkerque to Holland, unfortunately for him however, an early blast of arctic air froze the port of Rotterdam and his ships for the winter. Napoleon's plans were now jeopardy: his brother-in-law and half the French army in Saint Domingue were dead, rebel slaves had stopped shipping sugar and coffee to France, and Dutch ice stopped his army from taking Louisiana. "Damn sugar, damn coffee, damn colonies," Napoleon ranted.[55]

Napoleon tried again for the last time to put his plan in motion in the spring of 1803. He amassed troops at Brest and Rotterdam to sail to Saint Domingue, British spies however believed that their destination was England. On March 2, 1803, George III warned Parliament that "considerable military preparations are carrying on in the ports of Holland and France. . . ." The British responded by threatening war if the French fleets left port and entered the English Channel. Rather than risk so many lives, Napoleon abandoned the Louisiana expedition and decided to sell the territory to the Americans in order to buy arms for the possible next war with Britain.

"I renounce Louisiana, " Napoleon sadly declared. "I renounce it with the greatest regret. . . .I think of ceding it to the United States."[56]

"Through no effort of their own," the British ambassador in Paris said of the situation, "the Americans. . . .are now delivered."[57]

---

54 *Ibid.*

55 *Ibid.*

56 Maurice Denuziere, JeTeNommeLouisiane: Decouverte, colonisation et vente de la Louisiane (Paris: Editions Denoel, 1990),p. 393

57 Alexander DeConde, The Affair of Louisiana, p. 137

Epilogue

The Treaty of Mortefontaine and American Politics

With the signing of the Treaty of Mortefontaine, the Quasi War with France came to an end, except for its consent by the Senate of the United States. While the war was in progress, John Adams had a contentious relationship with members of his own Federalist party. A major cause was in sending a delegation to Paris in an effort to resolve the differences between the two nations and especially during the aftermath of the XYZ Affair when the treatment of the American ministers came to light.

One Federalist who did not constantly criticize Adam's policies in regard to France was Alexander Hamilton. He supported the president's decision to send the delegation to Paris in 1797 because he believed that a peaceful solution was preferable to war. Even after the XYZ Affair, Hamilton joined with Adams in adopting a policy of military preparedness with a willingness to negotiate. This military preparedness was a benefit to Hamilton because with aging George Washington appointed as commanding general, Hamilton's position as inspector general, would rank him as second in command, affording him considerable influence and prestige.

When Adams sent a second delegation to France, many Federalists believed that nothing had changed to warrant a new round of talks, but again, Hamilton's reaction was more moderate, only advocating a more cautious policy of delaying until the French government achieved greater stability, writing that "the [o]pinions of our people demand an accommodating course."[1]

The reaction to the treaty was not as moderate among Federalist senators where the party controlled twenty of the thirty-two seats. James Hillhouse of Connecticut found it "far short of what we had a right to hope or [expect]." Most Federalists went further, agreeing that the Convention was a shocking diplomatic defeat and an affront to national honor which would only be ratified with substantial modifications. The provisions of the treaty so astounded some of them that they wondered as Oliver Wolcott, also of Connecticut, if Oliver "Ellsworth's[2] mind ha[d] been enfeebled by sickness."[3]

Much of the Federalist press was equally hostile. the Boston *Columbian Centinel* was initially in favor of the treaty, however as opposition increased, the newspaper expressed hope that the Senate would agree that the treaty was "injurious to American honor and interests." According to the editor, "this humiliating convention" achieved only "dishonor" and "national humiliation" for the United States. Adding that "if the war continues and Great-Britain is disposed to resist our conduct, we have gained and merited hostility for the sake preferring peace."[4] Philadelphia's *Gazette of the United States & Daily Advertiser* feared that the failure to resolve "former misunderstandings" between the United States and France had resulted in a treaty that was a "shameful degradation of our country" and an "insolent triumph of France."[5] *The United States Chronicle*, published in Providence, encouraged the Senate to eliminate the objectionable portions of the treaty,[6] while the *Salem Gazette* maintained that there were several provisions "which an independent and spirited nation

---

1   Alexander Hamilton to John Marshall, October 2, 1800

2   One of the American ministers.

3   Oliver Wolcott to Thomas Pickering, December 28, 1800

4   *Columbian Centinel*, January 3, 1801

5   *Gazette of the United States & Daily Advertiser*, December 24, 1800

6   *United States Chronicle*, January 15 and 23, 1801

cannot submit to without disgrace and humiliation."[7] One of the few exceptions to this denunciation of the convention was the reaction of the *Massachusetts Spy,* a moderate Federalist newspaper in Worcester, which expressed relief that peaceful Franco-American relations had been restored.[8]

Republican newspapers were generally more supportive of the treaty. *The National Intelligencer and Washington Advertiser* and Philadelphia's *Aurora-General Advertiser* praised it for resolving the nation's difficulties with France peacefully. The former concluded that the nation should "rejoice in an honorable termination of disputes that hazarded its tranquility at home, and disturbed its relations abroad." The more partisan *Aurora-General Advertiser* compared the treaty to Jay's treaty, reporting that it was significantly different and better: It must be good, when it differs from all that was weak, disgraceful, ignorant, and ruinous."[9]

Although pleased that the undeclared war with France had ended, the Republican elected officials demonstrated little enthusiasm for the treaty. Even Thomas Jefferson expressed dissatisfaction. Believing that the treaty would not pass the Senate, he described it as the result of a "bungling negociation" with "some disagreeable features."[10] Like the Federalists, the Republicans doubted that the Senate would consent to the treaty without substantial alterations. The Republicans however agreed with George Washington about not having "entangling alliances" and therefore supported the suspension of the treaties of 1787.

The treaty's two greatest advocates were Adams and Hamilton. The president's support was understandable. He had endangered his political career and the unity of his party by sending a second

---

7   *Salem Gazette,* January 2, 1801

8   *Massachusetts Spy,* November 12 and December 24, 1800

9   *Aurora-General Advertiser,* January 8, 1801; *National Intelligencer and Washington Advertiser,* November 17, 1800.

10   Jefferson to Madison, December 19, 1800

delegation to Paris in an attempt to end the war. And when his diplomatic initiative succeeded, he believed that the convention was a significant achievement because it avoided an expanded war and allowed the United States to now establish relations with both England[11] and France "on a footing of equality." That policy was, Adams described it, "the precise point of Wisdom for us to aim at."[12]Although personal animosities prevented Hamilton from openly cooperating with Adams, he promoted unconditional ratification as energetically as the president. This response should not have been unexpected. Hamilton had occasionally supported Adam's policies toward France in the past,[13]and like the president he believed that the treaty was advantageous to the United States because of the abolishment of the earlier Franco-American treaties. He was also less concerned than other Federalists about how Great Britain would react and he believed that the American people preferred peace.[14]However, he also believed that the treaty was not without flaws and expressed a distaste for the convention saying that in "the general politics of the world" it "is a make-weight in the wrong scale," but he favored its approval because in view of the present state of public opinion its rejection would "utterly ruin the federal party and endanger the internal tranquility." Furthermore, he believed "it is better to close the thing where it is than to leave it to a Jacobin to do much worse."[15]

Domestic political considerations also affected Hamilton's opinion. He was apprehensive about what would happen during this increased "mania" for France, if the Federalist controlled Senate failed to act. Another reason for the Federalists to act and quickly was that not only did a Republican, Thomas Jefferson, defeat John Adams for the presidency, but also that the Senate would now be controlled by

---

11 Because of Jay's treaty

12 John Adams to Thomas B. Adams, January 27, 1801(Thomas B. Adams was John Adams' youngest son)

13 He agreed with Adams that a second delegation should be sent to Paris, even after the problems with the first one.

14 Alexander DeConde, *The Quasi War*, p. 289

15 *Ibid.*

the Republicans after Jefferson took office in March 1801. Hamilton also maintained that if the treaty were ratified it would demonstrate that the Federalists had "steered the vessel [of state] through all the storms . . . .into a peaceful and safe port." Sensitive to the misgivings of Federalists in the Senate, he hoped that they would express their reservations but "not withhold their assent."

The Federalists were also concerned about the effect the treaty would have on foreign affairs. Despite the opinions of their leadership, many Federalists were uneasy about the potential effect of the treaty on relations between the United States and Great Britain. Some feared that granting French privateers access to American ports and accepting a liberal definition of the commercial rights of neutrals might antagonize the British government. Article VI of the convention, which granted French privateers most-favored-nation status, seemed to some to be incompatible with the provisions of Jay's treaty.[16] In that agreement, the United States had granted British privateers and their prizes access to American ports and denied that right to anyone having "made a Prize upon the Subjects or Citizens of either of the said Parties." In addition, the previous treaty prohibited both nations from making "any Treaty that should be inconsistent" with this provision.[17]

Defenders of the convention attempted to alleviate these apprehensions. Rufus King, the American minister to Great Britain, reported that the British government had found no "ground for complaint" and determined that nothing in the convention was in conflict with Jay's treaty.[18] In addition, Adams sent a letter to the members of the Senate in which he reviewed the opinions of: Emmerich de Vattel, Hugo Grotius, and Samuel Pufendorf, leading scholars of international law, who all agreed that when a conflict existed between two treaties, "the more ancient has the advantage."

16 John Marshall to Alexander Hamilton, January 1, 1801

17 Treaty of Amity, Commerce and Navigation, between His Britannick Majesty; - And the United States of America, November 19, 1794, 12:28-29, (Jay's treaty)

18 Rufus King to the Secretary of State, October 31, 1800

Thus according to Adams' interpretation, the new treaty with France would not void the earlier agreement with Great Britain; rather, French privateers and their prizes would enjoy most-favored-nation status only after the expiration of Jay's treaty.[19] Hamilton also tried to assure his party members that there was no contradiction between the British and French treaties. He maintained that Great Britain had no reason to complain that the United States had granted that right to French privateers, because the British had gained the privilege prematurely when the Franco-American treaties were abrogated. Like Adams, Hamilton concluded that the British had "the advantages of priority" until the Jay treaty expired. Hamilton did not anticipate that the British government would react adversely to the new Franco-American accord, because of the domestic difficulties that plagued Britain at this time,[20] and given the entire situation Hamilton believed that a "good understanding with the United States is more than ever necessary to Great Britain."[21]

Despite Adams's belief that his arguments had been sufficient to satisfy the Federalists in the Senate, some remained skeptical and demanded more guarantees.[22] First, they wished to have the following wording added (which would make it virtually identical to Jay's treaty), "that nothing in this convention shall be construed as to operate contrary to any former and existing treaties." Secondly, they wished to have an eight year limit on the treaty. Both proposals passed with nearly unanimous bipartisan support.[23]

Hamilton did not believe that these additional proposal were necessary. There would be no "Perpetual Peace," he argued; war

---

19 John Adams to the United States Senate, January 21, 1801

20 During the year 1800 in Britain: George III survived two assignation attempts, An Act of Union was passed in Parliament connecting Great Britain and Ireland because of the Irish Rebellion in 1798, and inflation reached an all time high of 36.5%.

21 Hamilton to Morris, October 8, 1800

22 John Adams to Thomas B. Adams

23 United States Senate Executive Journal 1:366-67, 369, 370

would eventually cut "the knot" and allow the United States to reassess its relationship with France and be "free to renew or not, to renew absolutely or with qualifications."[24]Two Republican newspapers agreed. Washington's *National Intelligencer* and the *Virginia Argus* of Richmond argued that an additional article disclaiming conflicts with earlier treaties was superfluous. Both papers concluded that "the same effect would be produced without it, that would be produced by it.[25]

Many Federalists critics also feared that those sections of the convention delineating neutral rights would disrupt Anglo-American relations. Defining these rights liberally, they believed, would facilitate Napoleon's attempts to create a league of armed neutrals to offset British domination of the seas. Even if the United States never joined the league, Napoleon could cite inclusion of these provisions in the Convention of 1800 as indicative of American sympathy.[26]Federalist Senator Uriah Tracy of Connecticut believed that stipulations would lead to a war with Great Britain, because the United States seem to be aligning itself with other nations in challenging the British definition of neutral rights. Another Federalist senator, William Bingham of Pennsylvania argued that acceptance of these portions of the treaty required the United States "to protect the liberty of the seas." The English, he warned, would "resist the Principle or perish in the attempt."[27]

The treaty's supporters tried to allay these concerns. Hamilton conceded that the treaty's definition of neutral rights "will not be pleasant to the British Cabinet," but he supported the right of governments to negotiate treaties favorable to their interests. Suggesting that the American intent was not hostile toward Great

---

24 Hamilton to Morris, January 10, 1801

25 *National Intelligencer,* January 26, 1801: *Virginia Argus,* February 3, 1801

26 Arthur A. Richmond, "Napoleon and the Armed Neutrality of 1800: A Diplomatic Challenge to British Sea Power," *Journal of the Royal United Service Institute,* (May, 1959), p. 186-192

27 Salem Gazette (Massachusetts), February 27, 1801

Britain, Hamilton urged ratification. Although an attempt to exclude the article discontinuing the search of convoys failed to attract much support in the Senate, the partisan *Aurora-GeneralAdvertiser* declared that the motion betrayed "a spirit subservient to Britain and injurious to the rights of America, that is truly shocking."[28]

Objections to the treaty were not limited to its potential effect on Anglo-American relations; Federalists also criticized the convention for not resolving outstanding differences between the United States and France. During the negotiations that culminated in the convention, the French government refused to consider indemnification for private American ships unless the United States revoked its abrogation of the earlier (1778) treaties. Unable to resolve their differences, the negotiators agreed, in Article II, to defer resolution of the claims issue as well as the status of the previous Franco-American agreement into the future.[29] Senator Tracy maintained that French actions during the 1790s had annulled the treaties. Gouverneur Morris and other Federalists, certain that France would never indemnify the United States, and concerned that mere mention of the treaties would recognize their continued existence, preferred to have Article II excluded. Resisting appeals to party unity and peace, Morris maintained that an even greater issue was at stake. "So long as those Treaties (1778) shall exist America will not be completely independent."[30] Senator Hillhouse concurred: "The honor & Interest of this Country *forbids*" the restoration of an entangling alliance. Unlike Morris, however, Hillhouse and some newspaper editors also criticized the decision to abandon the claims, which were estimated up to $30 million. Acquiescing in the loss of indemnification and the "Sacrifice . . . .of *national honor,*" Hillhouse asserted, was tantamount to admitting that other countries "may plunder our merchants with *impunity.*"[31]Resolution of the claims

---

28 *Aurora-General Advertiser*, January 30, 1801

29 Pickering to Wolcott, January 3, 1801

30 Morris to Hamilton, January 5 and 16, 1801

31 *Columbian Centinel*, November 19, 1800

issue had been a sine qua non in the instructions to the American ministers; Davie, Ellsworth, and Murray. Hillhouse and the other New England senators considered its deferral a betrayal.[32]

Both Adams and Hamilton tried unsuccessfully to moderate these fears. The president admitted that the claims controversy was "the most mortifying thing & the only one painful to me," but he argued that the convention was otherwise "perfectly consistent" with the nation's honor and interests. Elimination of Article II or rejection of the entire treaty, Adams cautioned, would be even less advantageous.[33] Hamilton did not believe that the lack of indemnification was sufficient to defeat the treaty either. He concluded that the "price is not too great" to relinquish American claims in return for other benefits. The principal advantage, of course, was the status of the earlier Franco-American treaties. Hamilton maintained that their unilateral abrogation by the United States was only "a litigious right" and not secure until both nations concurred. In his opinion, Article II implied that the French agreed to leave the previous treaties inoperative "unless they shall be revived by the *consent* of the United States."[34] Once again, the arguments of Adams and Hamilton had little perceptible effect on their party's supporters in the Senate. During the initial period of the debate, all but three of the Federalists consistently voted to delete the second article while nearly all of the Republican minority voted to retain it.[35]

Article III was also a cause of apprehension among Senate Federalists. This article stipulated that all "public ships"[36] seized by either country before ratification of the treaty were to be returned.

32 Alexander De Conde, *The Quasi War*, p.186

33 John Adams to Thomas B. Adams, January 16 and 30, 1801

34 Hamilton, "France and America" October 8, 1800, in Harold C. Syrett (ed.) The Papers of Alexander Hamilton, 25:138-139. Before the treaty reached the United States, Hamilton suggested that the American government should compensate its own citizens for the indemnities so as to avoid the reassertion of the 1778 alliance.

35 Senate Executive Journal 1:365-366, 368

36 Merchant ships

Some Federalists believed that this provision was humiliating because the United States, if they seized French public ships during this period, would be forced to return them, while the French would not be forced to return the hundreds of American ships seized during the war. The Federalist senators also argued that it was more than the value of the ships that was at issue, that returning French ships would constitute an admission of aggression by the United States. They also objected to "*humbling* ourselves at the feet of France."[37] Former Secretary of State Timothy Pickering and Leven Powell, a Federalist congressman from Virginia agreed. Pickering feared that returning French vessels indicated that the war with France had been unjustified. Powell supported this view, arguing that Article III was "certainly degrading to this Country" because "it gives the appearance that we were the Aggressors."[38]

In response to this criticism, Adams and Hamilton contended that although restoration was "unpleasant," the provisions of the article were reciprocal. Hamilton also reminded the senators that the United States would continue to be abused by belligerents until it had become strong enough to "warrant higher pretentions." He did not believe that this article was so detrimental that the entire treaty should be rejected.[39] William Vans Murray, one of the American negotiators who was instrumental in constructing the treaty argued that because a state of war never existed, the United States could not refuse to return the French vessels. "The real glory was in *taking* them" anyway; to restore them would "show that though we value their friendship we have little cause to dread their maritime enmity."[40] Again the treaty's defenders seemed to have little effect. senators Hillhouse and Tracy, for example, rejected the contention that Article III guaranteed reciprocity. They continued to complain that the treaty did not require France to return or indemnify those

---

37 Alexander De Conde, The Quasi War, p. 289

38 Pickering to Wolcott, January 3, 1801

39 Hamilton to Morris, January 10, 1801

40 Murray to John Quincy Adams, February 10, 1801

American private vessels that had been seized.[41] Most Federalists voted to exclude Article III, when ever such a motion was introduced.

Burdened with a large number of proposed amendments and deletions, the Senate appointed a special committee to combine the various issues into a single proposal. The committee composed of two Federalists - Gouverneur Morris of New York and Jonathan Dayton of New Jersey - and one Republican - Wilson Cary Nicholas of Virginia - recommended that the Senate consent to the Convention of 1800 with four modifications: the rejection of the second and third articles and the addition of two new articles, one which would limit the duration of the treaty to eight years and the second which would state that nothing in the treaty was intended to conflict with earlier obligations.

In early January 1801, the Senate considered the committee's recommendations. Although most Republicans had earlier supported several of these proposals, they now refused to accept any modification other than the one limiting the duration of the treaty to eight years. Additionally, three Federalists; Humphrey Marshall of Kentucky, Raymond Greene of Rhode Island and Samuel Livermore of New Hampshire voted with the Republicans. In separate votes, the Senate decided to retain Articles II and III, limit the duration of the treaty to eight years, and reject the addition of a statement concerning previous treaty obligations.

On January 21, Adams gave the Senate a report from Edward Thornton, the British minister to the United States, who after examining the treaty stated that "the United States seems to have acquired no advantage but that of being freed from the burthensome stipulations of the Treaties of 1778, particularly the guarantee of the French West India possessions. Thinking men may allow this advantage to have been cheaply purchased by the abandonment of the claim of indemnity for the depredations of French Privateers." He

41 Hillhouse to John Trumbull, January 4, 1801. John Trumbull was an American artist during the Revolutionary war era and was notable for his historic paintings. He has been called "The Painter of the Revolution."

also stressed "the impatience with which at least the Merchants await its ratification, that intercourse with France may be renewed."[42]Adams also sent to the Senate a statement of the British Secretary of State for Foreign Affairs, Lord Grenville sent to him by the American minister, Rufus King, that after examining the treaty he found "no animosity nor unusual prejudice against us."[43]

Along with these reports about the British opinions of the convention, Adams also told the Senate "Although our right is very clear to negotiate treaties according to our own ideas of right and justice, honor and good faith, yet it must always be a satisfaction to know, that the judgments of other nations, with whom we have connection, coincides with ours."[44]

Adams' pressure did not work. Two days later the Senate rejected the convention. Although the agreement received 16 favorable votes as opposed to 14 nays, it failed to obtain the two-thirds majority. All the Republican senators voted for ratification and all but five Federalists voted against it. Gouverneur Morris reported that the treaty had been defeated "by the intemperate passion of its friends," but others maintained that party differences had caused the defeat. Within three days, Morris added that there was a general desire in the House of Representatives "to recede from the vote as it stands on the convention. As I all along suspected, it will be reconsidered.

Adams had tried to use his influence to get the amended convention ratified so that as Timothy Pickering wrote "his mighty mission might not end in a nullity."[45]Unfortunately for the

---

42 Thornton to Grenville, January 16, 1801

43 Rufus King to the Secretary of State. King also told William Vans Murray that the British saw no cause for complaint in the convention, and Murray wrote to John Quincy Adams that "it is a glorious thing for the administration to have put an end to hostilities with France, and yet have extorted the satisfaction of Great Britain., Murray to John Quincy Adams, November 18, 1800.

44 Adams to the Senate, January 21, 1801

45 Pickering to King, February 17, 1801

president, his influence was far too limited.[46] Pickering's assessment that the "highly improper" pressure exerted "on the *weaker brethren*" of the Federalist party was responsible for the defeat of the select committee's recommendations was, however, inaccurate.[47] As Senator Gunn was absent during that day's voting, unanimity among the Federalists would have accounted for enough votes to exclude only Article II, because that was the only one of the three defeated motions to attract a Republican vote. The proposed elimination of Article III and the inclusion of a statement on prior treaty commitments would not have attracted the necessary two-thirds majority without support from a least one Republican senator.[48]

Reaction to the Senate's rejection of the treaty varied. Hillhouse and Morris blamed the Republicans who "came out against modifications which had been agreed upon and insisted on the total rejection of the treaty."[49] The senate's action "extremely irritated" Adams, additionally, merchants and farmers who stood to profit from the renewed Franco-American trade were also disappointed.[50] Not everyone was displeased however, several Federalist newspapers praised the senators and thanked them, "Well done good and faithful servants."[51]

Adams's anger so discouraged Federalists from discussing the treaty with him that even Secretary of State John Marshall was unaware of the president's intentions, this also applied to his eldest son, John Quincy Adams, who wrote this about the vote, "For although it did not secure us what we ought by good right to have obtained, I am afraid we shall never get anything better, and that the longer settlement is delayed, the greater our damage will

---

46 While Adams was still president when the vote took place, he was a lame duck. Thomas Jefferson would become president on March 4, 1801

47 Pickering to his son John Pickering, February 5, 1801

48 Senate Executive Journal 1:313

49 Hillhouse to Trumbull, January 23, 1801

50 *Raleigh Register and North-Carolina State Gazette,* February 3, 1801

51 *Columbian Centinel,* February 4, 1801

be."[52]Some observers predicted that the treaty would be reconsidered and approved later with some modifications. [53] Others suggested that Adams call a special session of the new senate in early March before Jefferson became president and after several of the senators who voted against the convention had left office.[54]

Apparently concerned that rejection of the accord was contrary to the wishes of the American public, some Federalists supported a resolution to reintroduce it. Albert Gallatin, a Republican congressman from Pennsylvania, reported that several Federalist senators were willing to reverse their earlier vote if "afforded a decent cover." The Republicans were cooperative and negotiations for reconsideration began immediately. "However bad it is," one Federalist critic wrote, "a worse one may be made by the approaching administration; and no better one can be obtained by any administration." Although Senator Tracy doubted whether the Republicans could manufacture "some means to make us swallow it." a compromise was soon reached. Evidently, the Republicans agreed to support the exclusion of Article II (which deferred resolution of the status of the previous treaties and indemnification of claims) and the addition of a provision limiting the duration of the treaty to eight years, if the Federalists voted for the treaty as amended.[55] On February 3, 1801, the senate reconsidered the select committee's recommendations. In a demonstration of good faith, all the Republicans joined the Federalist majority to reject Article II by a vote of thirty to one. Only Federalist Humphrey Marshall dissented. A motion to eliminate Article III, which required the restoration of public ships, failed to attract the votes of two-thirds of the senators present. The senate then voted twenty-two to nine to ratify the treaty without Article II and with the addition of an article limiting the convention's duration to eight years after the exchange of ratifications. Eleven Federalists joined

---

52 John Quincy Adams to Rufus King, March 7, 1801

53 Thomas B. Adams to John Adams, February 2, 1801

54 Hillhouse to Trumbull, February 2, 1801

55 Albert Gallatin to Hannah Gallatin, February 5, 1801

eleven Republicans in the affirmative. Nine Federalists still found the convention unacceptable.[56]Stevens T. Mason, a Republican senator from Virginia, gleefully noted the dismay of those "Anglo-feds." "Nothing," he stated, could equal their "chagrin & mortification . . . .at having a French war once more snatched out of their hands and finding themselves sunk down to a minority of nine out of 31."[57]

Still convinced that portions of the treaty were "*dishonorable* and *disadvantageous* to our own Country," the nine Federalists who voted against ratification also wanted to eliminate Article III and add a stipulation disavowing conflicts with earlier treaty obligations. Morris would have accepted the convention as "not a bad Bargain" if the Senate had also rejected Article III. Arguing that it was wrong to "permit Profit or Convenience to stand in Competition with Honor," he feared that restitution might "damp[en] the Spirit of our Country." Still anxious about Great Britain's reaction, Tracy and Hillhouse demanded even more changes besides the elimination of Article III. They also insisted upon the addition of a clause clarifying conflicts with Jay's treaty and the removal of the "specious" and "impractical" rights of neutrals.[58]

Even after the senate ratified the convention, some Federalists in the House of Representatives tried to undermine Franco-American relations. In February 1800, Congress had suspended American commerce with France and its colonies until March 3, 1801.[59]Several weeks before that date, the House Committee on Commerce and Manufactures recommended that trade be suspended for another year. Republican opponents of the proposal, including Gallatin, Thomas T. Davis of Kentucky, Samuel Smith of Maryland, Edward Livingston of New York, and Virginians Joseph Eggleston and Henry Lee, argued that an extension was unnecessary. They maintained that senate ratification of the Convention of 1800 had resolved the

56 Senate Executive Journal 1:376-11

57 James Mason to James Monroe, February 5, 1801

58 Morris to Robert R. Livingston, February 20, 1801

59 The last day of the Adams' administration.

outstanding differences between the United States and France. The southerners in this group also reminded their colleagues that the cessation of trade had adversely affected the livelihoods of tobacco farmers and merchants. Smith suggested that northern shipping interests had not been similarly affected because they had been able to contract alternate cargoes.[60]

Federalist supporters of continuing the suspension, such as John Rutledge, Jr. of South Carolina, James Bayard of Delaware, Robert Waln of Pennsylvania, and Chauncey Goodrich of Connecticut argued that while France was considering the Senate's modifications of the convention, the United States should maintain a position of Strength and "preserve our national honor." The reestablishment of normal commercial relations should, therefore, be withheld to gain concessions from the French.[61]

On February 10, 1801, the House of Representatives voted fifty-nine to thirty-seven not to extend the suspension of trade between the United States and France. Federalists cast all of the thirty-seven minority votes; forty-three Republicans and sixteen Federalists comprised the majority. All but one of these sixteen Federalists represented a slave state.[62]Sectional economic interests affected partisan loyalties. Many southerners, who had earlier supported Federalist policies, now seemed eager to restore commercial relations with France.

Apparently the strongest influences in causing the Federalist legislators to change their votes was the general popularity of the convention, and the pressure of the mercantile interests which wanted to end the Quasi War because it injured business. International trade and shipping pumped life blood into American economic development at this time, and was at the heart of a prosperity which

---

60 *Annals of Congress.* 6th Cong., 2d sess., 1011-12. 1013-14.1015, 1017-18

61 *Ibid.,* 1013

62 Although New Jersey did not begin the process of abolishing slavery until 1804. It has been counted here as a free state.

the war had interrupted. Merchants wished to resume this trade but needed peace to do so.[63]

Following its ratification by the Senate, the convention was resubmitted to the French government. The French were not opposed to limiting the duration of the treaty, but they were concerned about the exclusion of Article II. They feared that consenting to its elimination implied their acceptance of the American abrogation of the treaties of 1778, but allowed the United States to reintroduce the claims issue later. The stalemate was finally resolved when one of the American negotiators, William Vans Murray, accepted a French proposal to have both governments "renounce the respective pretensions" to the previous treaties and the claims. With this modification, the Senate again consented to the Convention of 1800 in December 1801.[64]

Outside the Senate, economic interests caused some Federalists to agree with Adams and Hamilton on the benefits of the treaty. Two major sources of support were agricultural areas, particularly in the south, and northern cities. Many southerners had been unwilling earlier to endure French insults and encouraged the president's efforts to defend American honor after the "XYZ Affair." Several years of depressed prices and reduced demand for their products, however, made them eager to reestablish traditional outlets for their agricultural exports and anxious to end unpopular wartime taxes. Never ardently pro-English, they preferred a policy that ensured American independence from all foreign entanglements.[65] Commercial interests in some northern cities also favored renewed trade with France. As an example, sentiment was so strong for the original treaty in Philadelphia, that the Chamber of Commerce protested the Senate's modification of the treaty because businessmen in that city hoped

63 Trade with France and her colonies had dropped from $20.2 million in 1795 to $3.2 million in 1799. Timothy Pitkin, *A Statistical View of the Commerce of the United States* (London: Forgotten Books, 2017), P. 250-252

64 Alexander De Conde, *The Quasi War*, p. 316-325

65 *Raleigh Register and North Carolina State Gazette,* December 16, 1800. Tobacco prices increased as soon as the treaty arrived in the United States.

that the treaty would be reconsidered and ratified without any alterations.[66]

American representatives abroad also proved to be staunch defenders of the convention. John Quincy Adams, the American minister to Prussia, praised what had been achieved, that peace had been restored and the United States had gained concessions from France without alienating Great Britain. Given the state of military preparedness and the nature of public opinion, the younger Adams believed that the convention was the most advantageous agreement that could have been achieved. Rejection the convention in hopes of negotiating one more favorable to the United States was unreasonable, he argued, and he urged that "the rigorous exaction of *justice*" be sacrificed "for the sake of *peace.*"[67] William Vans Murray and Rufus King also supported the treaty. Their positions abroad may have afforded these men a more cosmopolitan and realistic perspective on the treaty than most Federalists could achieve at home.

There seemed to be little unanimity among the treaty's opponents. Senators Uriah Tracy, James Hillhouse, and William Bingham "Anglo-Feds" who equated American interests with British interests and sought to maintain cordial Anglo-American commercial and diplomatic relations. They were hesitant to take any action that Great Britain might interpret as antagonistic and were also hostile towards France. Senator Hillhouse, for example, undoubtedly had reservations about signing a treaty with France, a country he had described as "an Infidel Nation" and a "Harlot."[68]John Adams referred to these Federalists as "old tories" and "british agents who call themselves federalists" and blamed them for disrupting his policies.[69]

Also opposed to the treaty were such men as Senator Gouverneur Morris, who hoped to defend the nation's honor, but maintain a

---

66 Thomas B. Adams to Abigail Adams, February 21, 1801

67 John Quincy Adams to Thomas B. Adams, March 21, 1801

68 Hillhouse to Trumbull, December 15, 1800

69 John Adams to Thomas B. Adams, January 14, 1801

policy independent of both France and Great Britain. Unlike Senators Tracy, Hillhouse, and Bingham, Morris was less concerned about England's reaction to the convention. He and other Federalists like him were committed to developing an American policy free "from all intimate Connection with any of the Powers of Europe." They remained suspicious of France and were prepared to reject any treaty which did not satisfy their sense of American interests.[70]

Senators James Schureman and Jonathan of New Jersey, William Hindman and John Howard of Maryland and Henry Latimer of Delaware comprised another faction. Although these senators had consistently opposed the treaty, they eventually voted to ratify it without Article II and with an eight year limit. Apparently they found that alternative preferable to no treaty at all.

Ultimately, Adams and Hamilton proved incapable of convincing enough Federalists to ratify the convention without modifications. Adams, who had tried to remain aloof from partisan politics and base his policies on his perception of the national interest, was unable to persuade many of his fellow Federalists of the paramount importance of peace and maintaining cordial but independent relations with both Great Britain and France. He wanted the United States to determine its own policy without being entangled in European military and political affairs. Consequently, he was willing to make some concessions if it meant tacit abrogation of the earlier Franco-American treaties, the restoration of amicable relations between the two nations, and the normalization of trade.[71] Again as a lame duck, Adams political capital had been spent by 1801 and also as the historian Manning Dauer noted, one of Adams greatest failings was his inability "to act as a mediator among groups and bring eventual agreement.[72]

70 Morris to James Leray, February 4, 1801. Leray was a French supporter of the American Revolution.

71 John Adams to Thomas B. Adams

72 Manning Dauer, *The Adams Federalists* (Baltimore: The Johns Hopkins University Press, 1968) p. 265

Alexander Hamilton was no more effective. His reaction to the treaty was based on partisan as well as foreign policy considerations. Hamilton believed that besides enhancing the position of the Federalist party by ending the Quasi War and normalizing Franco-American relations, ratification of the treaty was a significant diplomatic achievement. The bilateral suspension of the earlier 1778 treaties allowed the United States to pursue its foreign policy interests without interference from others.[73] His opinions had little effect on the majority of the Federalist party however, as even some of his most ardent supporters became disillusioned after his attempt to sabotage Adams's presidential campaign in 1800.[74] Robert Troup, an intimate of Hamilton's was not the only Federalist who now considered Adams to be an "unfit head of the party."[75]

In June of 1801, William Vans Murray arrived in Paris, sent by a new president, Thomas Jefferson and a new secretary of state, James Madison, to present the Senate's modifications to the treaty. The French did not object to the eight year limitation on the convention, but we unwilling to acquiesce to the abolition of Article II, doing away with the 1778 treaties, because the French believed that they would still be liable to the indemnities.

On July 31, 1801, Murray signed the convention abolishing Article II and renouncing the indemnification claims even though he

---

73 Hamilton to Morris, December 24, 1880

74 Hamilton supported the other Federalist candidate, Charles Cotesworth Pinckney. Also the unintended circulation of the *Letter from Alexander Hamilton, Concerning the Public Conduct and Character of John Adams, Esq. President of the United States* was considered a major factor in Adams's defeat. In the letter, Hamilton begins with this premise: "Not denying to Mr. Adams patriotism and integrity, and even talents of a certain kind, I should be deficient in candour, were I to conceal the conviction, that he **does not possess the talents** adapted to the administration of government, and that there are **great and intrinsic defects in his character**, which unfit him for the office of chief magistrate." The letter went on to criticize Adams from the time of the American Revolution to his presidency. The letter was circulated throughout the country by the Jeffersonians.

75 Troup to Morris, December 31, 1800. Troup was a Federalist senator and also a college classmate of Hamilton's.

did not have the power to abandon the claims. Several days later, he reported the details to Madison," Perfectly in the Dark as I am on the views of the Senate in repressing the Second Article, I can not know the Extent of the Responsibility which I have assumed in accepting the French Ratification. . . . I concluded it for the best to exchange, rather than break off-"[76]

When news of the ratification arrived in the United States, even so staunch a Federalist as Gouverneur was pleased. The amendments to the convention, he pointed out, "have the great and salutary effect of terminating our intimate alliance with France." From this result, he concluded "that the affairs of the First Consul are not very splendid. He would not otherwise let go his hold of us, for though we are but a feather in the great scale of power, yet when that scale is nearly poised the weight of the feather is something."[77]

On December 11, 1801, Jefferson sent the convention to the Senate for approval, because the original terms had changed, and because, since the merchants were unhappy over the loss of indemnities, he wanted to leave the treaty "on the shoulders of the senate to accept."On December 19, the Senate with 22 yeas and 4 nays resolved that the convention was fully ratified.

With this approval of the Senate, the first entangling alliance in the history of the United States was formally abolished. After four years of quarreling mixed with warfare at sea, an undeclared war between the United States and France officially ended.

---

76 Murray to James Madison, July 23, 1801

77 Murray to John Parrish, October 5, 1801. Parrish was a Quaker abolitionist and a proponent of native American rights.

Bibliography

Speeches, Debates, Journals, Magazines, Documents, Annals, Papers, and Dissertations

American State Papers, foreign relations (Washington, 1832), 11

Annals of Congress, 3rd Cong. 1st sess. p. 215 & 340

Baldrige, Edwin, "Talleyrand in the United States," Doctoral Dissertation, Lehigh University, 1963

A Century of Lawmaking for a New Nation: U.S. Documents and Debates, 1774-1875, The Revolutionary Diplomatic Correspondence, Volume 1, Introduction, Chapter 4, p. 43

French-American Relations in the Age of Revolution: From Hope to Disappointment (1776-1800), Speech given on February 3, 2003 by Marie-Jeanne Rossignol, Professor of American Civilization, University of Paris 7

Helvidius, no. 4, September 14, 1793

John Marshall Papers, Manuscript Division, Library of Congress

Journal Politique de Bruxelles, August 12, 1786

Koch, Adrienne and Henry Ammon, "The Virginia and Kentucky Resolutions: An Episode in Jefferson's and Madison's Defense of Civil Liberties," *William and Mary Quarterly,* 3d ser., vol.5, no. 2 (April, 1948), p. 147

Kurtz, Stephen G., "The French Mission of 1799-1800," *The Academy of Political Science,* 80, no.4 (December, 1965), p. 546

Lyon, E. Wilson, "The Franco-American Convention of 1800, *The Journal of Modern History*, Vol. XII, September, 1940, Number 3

Pacificus, no. 1, June 29, 1793

Recueil des loisconstitutives, Paris, 1778, "Making Sense of Presidential Restraint: Federalist Arrangements and Executive Decision Making Before the Civil War," *Presidential Studies Quarterly*, February 14, 2014

Richmond, Arthur A., "Napoleon and the Armed Neutrality of 1800: A Diplomatic Challenge to British Sea Power, *Journal of the Royal United Service Institute* (May, 1959)

Rufus King Papers, Huntington Library, San Marino, California

Selinger, Jeffrey S. "Making Sense of Presidential Restraint: Federalist Arrangements and Executive Decision Making Before the Civil War," *Presidential Studies Quarterly*, February 14, 2014

State Papers and Public Documents of the United States [Edited by T.B. Wait], Third Edition, Vol. 1, Boston, 1819, p. 18

Schaffel, Kenneth, "The American Board of War, 1776-1787, PhD dissertation, City of New York, 1938

Stinchcombe, William, "The Diplomacy of the WXYZ Affair," *William and Mary Quarterly* (34) p. 599

"The Colonial Robespierre:" Victor Hugues on Guadeloupe, 1794-1798, *History Today* 27 (November, 1977)

Thomas Pickering Papers, Massachusetts Historical Society, also Vol.35, #193

U. S. Congress, American State Papers, Documents, Legislative and Executive, of the Congress of the United States, 38 vols. (Washington: Gales and Seaton, 1832-61), Class VI, Naval Affairs, 1:5

Books

Adams, John, *The Works of John Adams, Second President of the United States With a Life of the Author,* Charles Francis Adams, ed., 10 Vols., Boston: Little Brown and Company, 1850, VIII

Albertone, Manuela and Antonio DeFrancesco (eds.), *Rethinking the Atlantic World: Europe and America in the Age of Democratic Revolutions,* London: Palgrave Macmillan, 2009

Allen, Gardner Weld, *Our Naval War With France,* Miami: Hard Press Publishing, 1909

Ammon, Henry, *The Genet Mission,* New York: W. W. Norton & Co., 1973

Bancroft, George, *History of the Formation of the Constitution,* New York: D. Appleton, 1882

Belote, T.T., *The Scioto Speculation and the French Settlement at Gallipolis,* New York: B. Franklin, 1971

Bemis, Samuel, *Jay's Treaty, A Study in Commerce and Diplomacy,* New Haven: Yale University Press, 1923

Bemis, Samuel, *The American secretaries of State and their Diplomacy,* New York: Cooper Square Press, 1927

Billias, George, *Elbridge Gerry, Founding Father and Republican Statesmen,* Columbus: McGraw-Hill, 1976

Canny, Donald L., *The Sailing Warships of the U.S. Navy,* Annapolis: Naval Institute Press, 2001

Chambers, William Nisbet, *Political Parties in a New Nation: The American Experience, 1776-1809,* Oxford: Oxford University Press, 1963

Chernow, Ron, *Alexander Hamilton,* New York: Penguin, 2004

Childs, F. S., *French Refugee in the United States, 1790-1800,* Baltimore: Johns Hopkins University Press, 1940

Clark, William Bell, *Gallant John Barry, 1745-1803: The Story of a*

Naval Hero of Two Wars, New York: Macmillan Company, 1938

Corwin, Edward S., *French Policy and the American Alliance of 1778*, Princeton: Princeton University Press, 1916

Dauer, Manning J., *The Adam's Federalists*, Baltimore: John Hopkins University Press, 1993

De Conde, Alexander, *Entangling Alliance*, Durham, North Carolina: Duke University Press, 1958

De Conde, Alexander, *The Quasi War: The Politics and Diplomacy of the Undeclared War WithFrance*, 1797-1801, New York: Charles Scribner's Sons, 1966

De Conde, Alexander, *The Affair of Louisiana*, New York: Charles Scribner's Sons, 1976

Donavan, Frank, *The John Adam's Papers*, New York: Dodd Mead & Company, 1965

Dull, Jonathan R., *The French Navy and American Independence: A Study of Arms andDiplomacy*, 1774-1787, Princeton: Princeton University Press, 1975

Echeverria, Durand, *Mirage in the West*, Princeton, Princeton University Press, 1968

Elkins, Stanley, *The Age of Federalism*, New York: Oxford University Press, 1993

Ellis, Joseph, *Founding Brothers: The Revolutionary Generation*, New York: Vintage Books, 2000

Ellis, Joseph, *After the Revolution: Profiles of Early American Culture*, New York: W.W. Norton & Company, Inc., 2002

Estes, Todd, *The Jay Treaty Debate, Public Opinion, and the Evolution of Early American PoliticalCulture*, Amherst, Mass., University of Massachusetts Press, 2006

Fauchet, Claude, *Elogecivique de Benjamin Franklin*, Paris, 1790

Foner, Philip, S,, *The Democratic-Republican Societies, 1790-1800: A Documentary Sourcebook of Constitutions, Declarations, Addresses, Resolutions, and Toasts,* Westport, Conn.: Greenwood Press, 1976

Footner, Geoffrey, M. *Tidewater Triumph: The Development and Worldwide Success of the Chesapeake Bay Pilot Schooner,* Centerville, Md.: Tidewater Publications, 1998

Ford, Paul Leicester, *Writings of Thomas Jefferson* The 10 vols., New York: Putnam, 1892-1899, 3

Gernade, Claude, *Jefferson and Hamilton: The Struggle for Democracy in America,* Boston: Houghton Mifflin, 1925

Harper, John, American Machiavelli, New York: Cambridge university Press, 2004

Harwell, Richard, *Washington, An Abridgement in one volume of the seven volume GeorgeWashington* by Douglas Southal Freeman, New York: Charles Scribner's Sons, 1986

Horseman, Reginald, *The Diplomacy of the New Republic,* 1776-1815, Arlington Heights, Illinois: Harlen Davidson, Inc., 1985

Hofstadter, Richard, *The Idea of a Party System: The Rise of Legitimate Opposition in the UnitedStates,* 1780-1840, Berkley: University of California Press, 1969

Huthe, H. and W. J. Pugh, *Talleyrand in America as a Financial Promoter,* 1794-1796, Washington: U. S. Government Printing Office, 1942

Jefferson, Thomas, J.P. Boyd, ed. *The Papers of Thomas Jefferson,* Princeton, Princeton University Press, 1950

Johnson, Angelo Ronald, *Diplomacy in Black and White: John Adams, Toussaint Louverture, andTheir Atlantic World Alliance,* Athens, Georgia: University of Georgia Press, 2014

Jones, Howard Mumford, *American and French Culture,* 1750-1848, Chapel Hill: University of North Carolina Press, 1927

Jones, Howard Mumford, The Course of American Democracy,

Danbury, Ct., Scholastic Library Publishing, 1985

Kaplan, L. S., *Colonies into Nations: American Diplomacy,* 1763-1801, New York: Macmillan, 1972

Kramer, Lloyd S. The French Revolution and the Creation of the American Political Culture in Joseph Klaits and Michael H. Haltzel eds. *The Global Ramifications of the French Revolution,* Cambridge: Cambridge University Press, 2002

Leiner, Frederick C., *Millions for Defense, The Subscription Warships of 1798,* Annapolis: Naval Institute Press, 2000

Lodge, Henry Cabot, *Life and Letters of George Cabot,* Boston: Little Brown & Co., 1878

Malone, Dumas, *Jefferson and the Ordeal of Liberty,* Boston: Little Brown & Co., 1963

Manning, J. Dauer, *The Adam's Federalists,* Baltimore: John Hopkins University Press, 1993

Markham, Felix Maurice Hippiel, *Napoleon,* New York: The New American Library of World Literature, 1963

Miller, John C., *The Federalist Era,* 1798-1901, New York: Harper & Brothers, 1967

Minnigerode, Meade, *Jefferson, Friend of France,* New York: P. Putnam & Son, 1928

Montague, Andrew J., *"John Marshall,"* The American Secretaries of State and Their Diplomacy, ed., Samuel Flag Bemis, New York: Alfred J. Knopf, 1927

Neilson, Jonathan M., *Paths Not Taken,* Westport, Ct.: Praeger, 2000

North, Douglas C., *The Economic Growth of the United States,* New York: W.W. Norton & Co., 1966

Lacour-Gayet, G., *Talleyrand,* Paris, 1928

Palmer, Michael, A., *Stoddert's War: Naval Operations During the Quasi War with France,* 1798-1801, Columbia, South Carolina:

University of South Carolina Press, 1987

Palmer, R. R., *The Age of Democratic Revolution: A Political History of Europe and America,* 1760-1800, (2 vols.)Princeton: Princeton University Press, 1959-1964, ii

Perkins, Bradford, *The First Rapprochement: England and the United States,* 1795-1805, Oakland: University of California Press, 1955

Perkins, James, *France in the American Revolution* Williamstown, Mass.: Corner House Publications, 2014

Pitkin, Timothy, *A Statistical View of the Commerce of the United States,* London: Forgotten Books, 2017

Poniatowski, Michael, *Talleyrand aux Etats-Unis,* 1794-1796, Paris: Presses de la Cite, 1967

Riquetti, HonoreGaberiel, *Comtede Mirabeau, Considerations sur L'Order de Cincinnatus,* London, 1784

Rossignol, Marie-Jeanne, *The Nationalist Ferment,* Columbus: The Ohio State University, 2004

Schachner, Nathan, *The Founding Fathers,* New York: A. S. Barnes & Company, 1954

Smelser, Marshall, *The Democratic Republic*: 1801-1815, New York: Harper Collins, 1968

Soules, Francois, *Historire des Troubles de l'Ameriqueanglaise* (1787), iv

Sprout, Harold & Margaret, *The Rise of American Naval Power,* 1776-1918, Princeton, Princeton University Press, 1944

Stinchcombe, William C., *The American Revolution and the French Alliance,* Syracuse: Syracuse University Press, 1969

Syrett, Harold, ed., *The Papers of Alexander Hamilton,* 44 Vols., New York: Columbia University Press, 1972, 16

Unger, Harlow Giles, *The French War Against America: How a Trusted Ally Betrayed Washingtonand the Founding Fathers,* Hoboken: John

Wiley & Sons, Inc., 2005

United States Navy Department, Office of Naval Records and Library, Naval Documents Related to the Quasi-War With France: Naval Operations, February 1797- December 1801, Dudley W. Knox, ed., 7 Vols., Washington, D. C., 1935-1938, 1, p. 175-176

Varg, Paul A., *New England and Foreign Relations,* 1798-1850, Hanover, New Hampshire: University Press of New England, 2002

Varg, Paul A., *Foreign Policies of the Founding Fathers,* East Lansing: Michigan State University Press, 1963

Wharton, Francis, *The Revolutionary Diplomatic Correspondence of the United States*, Government Printing Office, 1899, Volume ii

Index